COLORFULLY **CONSTRUCTED**

COLORFULLY
CONSTRUCTED

How God Builds His Kingdom with Unique Personality Colors

Rhonda L. Beckham, Debbie Mankin,
Cindy Patton, and Dr. T.D. Rogers

WordCrafts Press

Colorfully Constructed

ISBN: 978-1-952474-69-9

Cover concept and design by Megan Starling-Lamb.

Published by WordCrafts Press
Cody, Wyoming 82414
www.wordcrafts.net

Contents

Preface

I might have loved better if I had known what is in this book.

For some reason, I thought that people who processed the world differently than I do were *deliberately* trying to make my life hard. I'm a solid green: why would anyone choose a sappy feeling over a rock-solid fact? Why do people insist on small talk when there are a thousand secrets in the universe reserved for those who will just be quiet? And why must anything change—ever?

Yes, for years, stuck in a world filled with extroverted, impulsive, effervescent, small-talking, snuggling, consensus-building people, I assumed that there was a vast conspiracy determined to slowly drain my sanity.

Until I learned that people relate to the world differently. Those who live by lists actually enjoy ticking off items throughout the day. Spontaneous people actually love the adventure that comes from taking every minute at a time. And sentimental people actually feel most alive when they are loving on somebody else.

And all this time!

It shouldn't surprise us that the same God who made everything from quarks to supernova, from amoeba to kudzu, from fur to steel, also made humans from green to gold and from blue to orange. What is surprising is that some of us wander through life never fully appreciating that these differences are actually blessings. Regardless of which direction we might face, if we have all the colors in the room, we know what to do.

So when North Boulevard's Living Color team began taking their presentations on the road, I knew it would help people immensely. Our churches need training in how to love those who process the world differently. We need to know that blues and greens complement one another, as do oranges and golds. We need to learn that a body made of only hands, or only ears, or only knuckles, is a body that cannot flourish. You need every part of your body to win a race. You need all the colors of the palate to make a mosaic.

This book will help you understand why others act differently than you. It will help your marriage: your spouse *should* be different from you. It will help you raise your children: they are designed by God to process the world as they do. This book will help you love people better because you will know what feels like love to others. It will help you learn how better to encourage because you'll discover what motivates different people. And it will help you build your church team because you'll learn how to recruit from every color in order to accomplish the fullness of what God has set before you.

The old saying suggests that none of us is as smart as all of us. This would not be true if all of us were the same color. It is the divine blend of our variety that makes us strong.

So work your way through this book, asking not just "what color am I?" but also "how can I love *that* color better?" Ask which color can best implement this or that ministry. Stretch yourself by offering encouragement using the palate of another person's color. Celebrate what makes you different, knowing that where you are weak, God made another strong.

Mother Teresa is reported to have said that "none of us, including me, ever do great things. But we can all do small things, with great love, and together we can do something wonderful."

Get the colors right, and do wonderful things.

David Young
Senior Minister, North Boulevard Church
Murfreesboro, Tennessee

Laying The Foundations

Sit on a park bench for any amount of time, and it will become obvious. People are interesting. While we certainly have characteristics common to our species, we are also incredibly diverse in the way we think, communicate, and behave. Add to that our inherent desire to be social, and the diversity of interactions between people who may be similar or may be polar opposites is multiplied.

The diversity within God's creation includes a range of personality types. Often when we think about personality differences, we think of personality conflicts. This may be because we are underutilizing the strengths and differences that God has given us. Learning to capitalize on the differences will help every individual in building God's kingdom.

Background

Our interest in understanding ourselves and others is the likely basis for the ancient practice of attempting to categorize people into personality types. Even ancient philosophers like Hippocrates identified four personality types: Melancholic, Choleric, Phlegmatic, and Sanguine. More modern versions of personality inventories have been proposed and researched including the Myers-Briggs Type Indicator (MBTI) and the Big Five Personality Test. Research has often debated the accuracy and validity of these tests. In addition to the inherent difficulty of measuring abstract concepts like personality, researchers debate whether personality can change across time or circumstances. Personality tests also may not generalize across all populations of people. Additionally, major personality tests like the MBTI, for example, were not even created by professionals in the field. Instead, the MBTI was created by two housewives, Katharine Cook Briggs and her daughter, Isabel Briggs Myers. They based their test on their personal observations of people, both in life and in literary works. And yet these tools, though controversial, remain widely used in psychology and personality research.

A perfect test to categorize personalities may not be possible although we recognize the real need to create tools to better understand our own and others' tendencies and temperaments. If you have ever taken a personality test, you may recognize the usefulness of these tools. Insights into our personalities can help us to identify our personal strengths and weaknesses and can help us explain ourselves to others who might find our way of navigating life mystifying. Additionally, and perhaps even more importantly, we can better understand those around us by learning about their personality type. The condensed explanations of personalities provided by personality tests give us a quick glimpse into another's mind. We can better understand why they may behave or think the way they do and therefore better equip ourselves for interacting with them.

The issue we have found with many popular personality tests is that there are so many personality types that it becomes difficult to remember the characteristics of each type such that if a friend tells us that she is an INTP or an Enneagram 8, we may not be able to completely apply the information she has provided. It is just too difficult to have a ready understanding of each personality type when the inventory has nine, sixteen, or even more designations.

The Living Color assessment was created in order to classify personalities into four simple categories: Green, Orange, Blue, and Gold. Others have used four colors to identify personality categories in the past. By sorting personalities into four categories, the Living Color assessment is useful to identify your own personality and simple enough to identify and remember the other personality colors. In this way, the Living Color assessment becomes an excellent tool in work environments, churches, and small groups. By understanding *both* your personality color and the personality color of the people with whom you interact, you can create healthier group dynamics and more fully utilize the strengths of individuals within the group.

Creating The Living Color Assessment

"Let's take this show on the road," exclaimed Cindy Patton in the hallway of the school where she worked with Debbie Mankin. They had just been part of the school accreditation team directed by Lynne Maxwell. Any school that is accredited has to go through regular reviews of their practices by outside personnel assigned to the process. To prepare for the accreditation process, Lynne had decided to assign tasks to each member of the team based on personality colors. The school faculty and administration were given a color personality test created by a friend of Lynne's. Each person's assignment was designated based on the strengths associated with their personality color. The team worked particularly well together, and the accreditation process resulted in outstanding reviews for the school.

Later, Debbie, the school's guidance counselor, was asked to help the high school students determine their personality colors. She devised a simple ten-question test that helped the students reveal their color. After that, whenever a student was discussed, his or her color was mentioned to give everyone a frame of reference. A new language of color became part of the school's culture that teachers, administrators, and students understood and used. The color language gave the school a set of criteria that brought clarity to any discussion, whether it involved a student, a parent, or a fellow colleague. It became clear that they had found something that could be beneficial outside the walls of their school.

Unbeknownst to the three of them, this was the beginning of their color team. When Debbie was asked to teach a series of lessons for the women at her church, she remembered that Cindy and Lynne were each dominant in a color different from hers. They each presented a lesson explaining the common traits of their colors. Positive comments with lots of questions from the audience were received after each class. One of the women in the class had requested the series for her own understanding of how colors work for her, her mother, and her sister. After she discovered that she and her mother were the same color, the oldest sister declared that she now got why they understood each other but not her. The women went home after the classes to tell their husbands what they had learned and how it could be applied to their marriages. For the next few years, Cindy, Lynne, and Debbie traveled throughout Middle Tennessee presenting lessons about personality colors at church events and classes using the simplified personality questionnaire devised for use at the school.

In 2018, Debbie, Lynne, Cindy, and another friend who was dominant in the fourth color conducted classes for the women at the annual conference held at their church and explained the tool that they had been using to describe personality colors. Afterward, women from four different congregations approached them asking them to come present at their churches. With much prayer and direction from the Holy Spirit, the Living Color Conference was born. The four came together to devise their own original assessment and to develop their own unique materials and activities that would be used at each of the conferences. Their emphasis in their presentations was to show how each person's God-given personality could be used for Kingdom work.

About The Living Color Conference

The Living Color Conference was developed to be used in church settings as a one-day or two-day seminar for attendees to take a three-part personality color assessment, identify their personality color, learn about the others, and understand ways in which the colors can complement one another. To start each conference, all participants take the three-part assessment that provides a score for each of the personality colors. Scores on each personality color are then ranked to show their dominant color and their second color. Each person's highest score on the assessment represents their strongest personality color. However, no one is exclusively one color. Everyone has some of each color in differing amounts. The second highest color influences how the dominant color is displayed.

After participants have identified their first and second color, each member of the Living Color team gives a presentation to further explain her personality color. The members of the team have changed with time, but the commitment to have each color explained by a presenter who is strong in that color remains the same. The presenters offer core traits of each color, identify common strengths and weaknesses of each color, and give personal testimonies of their own experiences.

The conferences are designed so that you walk away with an understanding of your color and the ability to start you on your journey of appreciating the personality colors of those around you. We offer activities at our conferences that will deepen your perception of how the colors can work together. The conference simplifies personality into four distinct colors so that they can become a straightforward, easy-to-remember tool that can be applied in all interactions with others. This book is intended to be a supplement to our conferences and therefore does not include the assessment that we use. However, we do hope that you can determine what your dominant color is as you read the following chapters. More information about our Living Color team and how to organize a Living Color Conference for your group can be found at the website: www.livingcolorconference.com.

About The Book

As we have conducted our conferences over the years, we have had those in attendance ask if we have a book for them to read after our presentations. This book came about to supplement the conferences and to give the readers an introduction to what they may learn when they attend the conference. Personality theory can be used in any setting, but our focus has been to show how the four personality colors can bring a clearer understanding of how God constructed His Kingdom. God created each person with a unique personality, and He intended the four personality colors to complement each other and enhance the work of the church. This book is written by four people who are each dominant in one of the personality colors. We feel that the individual perspectives of the four authors can give you a better insight into how each color works rather than having one person tell you about all the personality colors. Each of the following four chapters that explains a personality color is written by an author who is strong in that color, and readers will find their personalities are even reflected in their writing styles.

When you come to an understanding of personality colors through this book, you will better understand several concepts. You have particular strengths and weaknesses based on your personality which will be different than others' but equally important. When you are in group settings, the groups can function better if you identify each person's strengths. We have found this to be useful in many group settings including family, work, and ministry.

From the green chapter, you will learn that greens base their thinking on logic and evidence, value competence, are ingenious problem solvers, and weigh every option to make the best possible decisions. From the orange chapter, you will learn that oranges base their thinking on creativity and freedom, value humor and optimism, are spontaneous and enthusiastic, and are energized by people. From the blue chapter, you will learn that blues base their thinking on feelings and intuition, value acceptance, are emotionally sensitive and avoid risk, and are quick to hug. From the gold chapter, you will learn that golds base their thinking on order and structure, value rule-following and fairness, are dependable and prepared, and like checklists to accomplish goals. Our aim is for you to learn about yourself but also to figure out the personalities of others in your life from the viewpoint of someone who has lived that color.

Building With The Green Personality

By Dr. T.D. Rogers

Simply, the green personality can be described as rational, logical thinkers. This is not to be confused with intelligence as everyone uses their "thinking" abilities, and we all have intelligence. However, when making decisions, greens are less likely than other colors to consider their emotions, subjective experience, or the impact on others, and they are more likely to use impersonal logic and objectivity. This emphasis on information and logic combined with a de-emphasis of interpersonal and emotional factors can create a manner of thinking, behaving, and socializing that can look very different from the other personality colors.

Thinking It Through

People with a green personality type are likely to enjoy learning and gaining new information. Greens are often avid readers and researchers. They are often good at identifying patterns and inconsistencies. While eating lunch one day, my oldest son held up a package of deli cheese and exclaimed, "This is so weird!" Confused, I asked what was strange about it, and he said, "This package has a zipper seal on the side. Most zipper seals are at the top. I think it makes the cheese come out easier." I laughed knowing that he is green like his mother and had noticed an exception in a pattern that interested him. He also deduced why it was that way. Greens often want to know why something is the way it is. The reasons why help to inform greens if something is working well or not. Unlike golds, greens don't value tradition and doing things the same way all the time. Greens are much more likely to test systems and determine new ways of doing things. Greens are often creative in this way and can create unusual solutions to problems. I remember my calculus teacher in high school asking me to meet with her before class one day. She asked how I had gotten the answers on my homework. I explained my answers to her, and she said, "But that's not how we went over it in class." I had gotten the same answer, but I had thought through the question in a completely different way. This was an early realization that I sometimes think through things in an unusual way. It certainly wouldn't be the last, but over time I have learned to value my difference of perspective.

Deliberately Delayed

Because greens take a long time to think and consider things, they often are often late to turn in projects, reply to emails, and arrive at meetings. I teach courses to university students nearly every day. Despite having taught the same courses for years, I find myself sprinting out of the office at the last moment having added what I think are important details and new additions. I haven't mis-planned my time but instead am unable to stop considering my presentation until required to. I am also often the last to speak up at meetings or to reply to long text chains. I want to integrate all the information presented and then weigh in with my thoughts. Greens want to be very careful not to act on impulse or emotion but instead approach everything with logic. An important part of logic is having all the relevant information, and so it becomes important to wait to understand all perspectives and gain all available information before replying to a group. Greens may also not be considering the personal impact of their lateness by thinking about making others wait or by considering the impact of their silence in group settings.

Inventive And Idealistic

I remember my mother once spouting off her Saturday plans to her mother as I, a teenager, overheard. She had a long list of household chores, gardening, errands in town, a couple of new sewing projects (which particularly excited her), and plans to cook dinner. My grandmother, always speaking just to the point, asked, "And how many days will it take you to finish Saturday?" My mother had planned far more than she could possibly complete in one day, and yet what struck me most was the thought, "Maybe that's why I never get everything done that I plan. Maybe I plan too much." Despite learning this lesson, I continue to create grand visions for almost everything. I recently planned to host a baby shower in my home and was planning out the decorations with a friend. She came over the day before the party and I presented her with my list. "We can do a balloon arch over here and banners over here and move the furniture around this way and...." My friend looked at me carefully and said, "Since the party is tomorrow, what do you think you'll have time for?" Even with her kind prompt, I still had a hard time limiting myself to only one or two things. This is a common struggle for me. I create a grand plan in my head.

However, the picture of the end result is only part of the fun. Problem-solving my way to reaching the goal is a challenge I enjoy. While oranges are also very creative, they may enjoy the process of brainstorming, trying many unexpected things, and discovering surprising results. Greens tend to have a very specific goal in mind that they think either improves something or poses a problem-solving challenge. I have plans to completely overhaul the college courses that I teach by incorporating a game or experiment. I can picture what I want students to learn, and I strategize on how to get them to that goal. I enjoy baking cakes as a hobby and will often view YouTube videos of professionals making their cakes and think, "What could I do to make a cake that looks similar?" However, it is inevitable that I don't get to all (or sometimes even most) of my plans. Reality sets in that I have limited time or limited energy to complete my vision. Greens are fantastic at exploring many possibilities or solutions. They enjoy thinking big and coming up with grandiose plans. They also enjoy complex problems and thinking of unusual solutions. Greens will want to try new things and brainstorm ideas. However, their plans and solutions may not be realistic. I once was tasked with making twenty-four ornaments for a church Christmas event. In true green fashion, I had thought and thought about what I was going to make. I wanted to make something really worthwhile. I planned right up to the day before I was supposed to bring them and finally committed to the idea and purchased the supplies to sew together felted ornaments. I sat down at my kitchen table that evening and began. I made the first one and timed myself to see how long it would take. To my surprise, given the time it took me to complete one, I would be sewing until 4:00 a.m. I have found that it is particularly important to have some gold friends and family in my life who can anchor me to reality. They help to anchor my excitement about my big plans to the reality of needing to be able to execute them.

Data-Driven But Not Disconnected

In their pragmatism, greens may be seen as selfish or disconnected. A green friend of mine is well known in his family for being unlikely to go with the group during family outings. On a family vacation, the entire family visited a museum. For a family of mostly blues, this was planned to be a social event. For this green family member, however, it was a learning experience. He visited every exhibit, carefully reading each caption along the way. He got farther and farther behind the rest of the family as they chatted and enjoyed each other's company. When the family had to wait on the green member to be done, they wondered why he was being such a loner and why he was making them wait. Greens may easily prioritize information over others' feelings or wants.

Greens may not express themselves emotionally. I personally find even my own strong emotions a bit overwhelming, much less the strong emotions of others. In college I clearly remember so many friends having big celebration moments—promising first dates, engagements, new jobs—and I really wanted to celebrate with them as they announced the big news to a throng of squealing friends. However, I could never manage to match the enthusiasm of the group and defaulted to asking about starting dates, wedding themes, and other factual (and therefore more comfortable) information. Marrying into a family of mostly blue personalities has further magnified my lack of emotional expression. My husband's family has large holiday events, and everyone that enters is greeted with an enthusiastic cheer and long hugs. I sometimes think I might melt under the pressure to perform this ritual. During annual Christmas gift exchanges, they take turns opening gifts to see everyone's reaction. Being raised in this environment, they have all had classic training in gift opening—make eye contact with the gift giver, explain that this is the only thing that you've ever wanted in your whole life, and tell them you love it while shedding a tear. They do this beautifully, and it is a clear demonstration of the love they have for each other. It is so sweet to watch. Until it's my turn. And then I sweat. I can't think clearly and misidentify the item or the gift giver. And worst of all I can't cry. Despite mentally acknowledging how thankful I am, I am unable to create this sentiment in emotional expression. My dry thank you is unconvincing.

Greens are notorious for this lack of emotional display and are often perceived as cold, indifferent, or detached. I have spent a considerable amount of time trying to understand why I am so uncomfortable with emotional expression (again with the importance of why). I certainly have emotions even if they are generally somewhat subdued compared to others. I have very sincere feelings of love, appreciation, and compassion. But so often I feel uncomfortable expressing them due to feeling awkward or feeling like I'll be perceived as insincere. Greens often see others' robust emotional displays as being trite social requirements. An enthusiastic, "This is the best meal I've ever had!" heard by a green person might trigger the recollection of all their favorite meals and a qualitative comparison.

Greens often feel uncomfortable receiving or giving praise for the same reason. Other colors might feel the need to praise something or someone out of a sense of obligation or not wanting to hurt their feelings. Greens may suspect that praise is insincere or inaccurate and overblown because of this. Greens often resist giving praise because they want the praise to be accurate. When my children hand me drawings, I will often identify elements of the drawing they have improved on instead of generally saying it's the most beautiful thing I've ever seen. I might say, "I can see you colored in the lines for that flower," for example. I feel that I'm providing accuracy and informative feedback when I do this.

Logically Literal

People with green personalities are often very literal. Greens often miss jokes or misinterpret figurative speech. Sometimes greens may answer very simple questions in unusually literal ways. At a recent gathering, some friends and I had laid out some snacks on a table and were sitting down to enjoy them together. One friend turned and asked, "Hey where did you get that fruit?" I had actually brought the fruit and so I quickly answered, "At the grocery store." She thought I was making a snarky joke and laughed as I quickly realized she meant for me to indicate where on the table the fruit was located. Common figurative phrases are also troubling for greens. I am constantly misquoting common metaphorical sayings. Instead of, "Don't look a gift horse in the mouth," I might say, "Don't give back a gift horse," as I try to logically deduce how the saying should go. My green son once observed that many homes have signs in them that say, "Home Sweet Home." He wondered aloud, "Why would the sign in someone's home say 'Home Sweet Home' instead of 'Home is where you're at right now?'" Interestingly, he didn't see the "sweetness" of a home being nearly as relevant as your physical location. I can't say I disagree.

Discerning With Distance

Greens are also notorious for not wanting physical touch except with a few people whom they know well. This can simply be due to a green person's tendency to be reserved in social settings. Greens generally avoid the limelight (except when giving information on a pet topic), and touching people may, in the green person's mind, attract unwanted attention or create an overly expressive delivery. However, many greens generally note that physical touch is reserved for people they know very well. A green might be overwhelmed with the warm and fuzzy hugs so generously given by blues. I am very physical with my children and husband frequently giving them hugs and kisses. Having two boys, it's impossible to get away without the occasional wrestling match as well. However, for people in public, I often find myself standing at a distance or avoiding even accidental touches. Touching someone you don't know can also be unpredictable and awkward. I remember standing at my wedding shower with a vigorous internal dialogue of how best to greet attendees. "Okay, I don't want to touch noses with this person, but they are clearly going to hug me—which way does my head go? Left or right?" A guessing game ensues of trying to predict whether each person will give a side hug, arm squeeze, or passing smile. What gesture to offer back fills most of my thoughts. Greens will often give subtle clues that they don't prefer to be touched such as keeping their distance or facing slightly away. These cues can be misinterpreted as disinterest or dislike if you don't recognize the green personality.

Not Indifferent, But Also Not Intuitive

Most people, during social situations, will use their intuition to understand what people are feeling and how they are experiencing their side of the interaction. Greens may conduct themselves in social situations quite differently. Many greens are introverted and may avoid group settings. At family gatherings, they may be the ones in the corner of the room with a book or their smartphone consuming most of their attention. Others may not want to be the center of attention but will enjoy observing a social setting. They may be listening to the conversation while not saying much. They may be interested in taking in the information provided by discussions but not very interested in contributing. Greens may even see simply being in a social situation as a type of participation. I once picked up my green son from aftercare at his school to find him playing at a table alone in a small room full of kids. I asked him why he was playing alone, and he looked at me with confusion. "I'm not. I'm playing with all of my friends," he answered while motioning around the room as if I had overlooked the twenty-seven kids running around.

When evaluating a situation or problem, greens are unlikely to think about the personal or emotional side of it. I have a group of female friends from church (yes, greens have friends), and one of them, Jen, recently had a baby. Jen experienced postpartum depression afterward and asked for help from the group. The blues and golds of the group immediately took action and formed a calendar for us to rotate sitting with her and bringing her and her family (her husband, three-year-old son, and now her newborn daughter) dinner. I signed up for a Thursday evening and spent the week thinking through what her day might look like and what challenges she may face when no one was there. So, I made muffins for breakfast so that she wouldn't have to worry about feeding everyone the next morning, and I purchased some toys to keep her son occupied.

On Thursday, I made my dish and headed over (a bit late of course because... well, I'm green). I saw that Jen was crying when I walked in, and I empathetically asked how she was feeling. Even though these big emotions made me a bit uncomfortable, I popped the dinner in the oven and came back to the living room to sit with her. Later, she told the group about the interesting differences in the care she received from different members of the group. She said that our blue friends had plopped down right next to her and given her a big hug. They cried with her, prayed with her, and talked through her emotions. I, however, had sat across from her on the other side of the sectional, observed her emotions, asked a few questions, and checked on dinner in the oven often. "Did I really sit on the other side of the room?" I thought as she retold everything. Of course, I had, but she was nursing a baby and experiencing sadness. I thought she would need space as I would. I thought that by sitting with her I was telling her I cared for her. "Perhaps I should have actually said that," I thought. This is an area of particular difficulty for me. It's hard for me to understand what others might need in emotional situations, whether they are times of sadness or celebration. I had spent lots of time thinking about Jen, but it may not have translated as I expected.

Similarly, my oldest, and very green, son had an experience trying to comfort his younger brother. My middle child is a six-year-old boy who is very blue, very relational, and who is often very hungry. Food is very important to him, and he asks daily what the school lunch will be. One evening my middle child did not like what we were having for dinner and was hurt that we did not plan to make him a separate, specially prepared meal that he would like. He ran up to his room crying. Our oldest child went to check on him and comfort him. My husband and I looked at each other, both thinking what an awesome job our oldest was doing to consider his brother despite his natural green tendency to ignore these big emotions. We then overheard him say gently, "Don't cry, buddy. If you don't eat, you'll starve to death." Green compassion may look a bit different, but we do care. When dealing with greens, it's important to remember that although they may seem socially disconnected, they may be considering other people in a very different way.

Liberated Not Limited

Greens enjoy independence when working and often when doing things that they enjoy as well. Again, greens may be introverted and may enjoy the energy renewal of solitude. Greens may also see organizing others as being one extra task when working in teams. Greens often have a clear picture of what the end result of a project or task should look like. Without the planning and organizing skills of golds, getting everyone else to execute a green's plans can be burdensome. It may even be seen by a green as a distraction from actual progress that they could be making on their own. Greens often don't want to take on the role of leader because of these factors. Instead, a green might opt to work alone. Greens will often measure their success against the end result that they had pictured, and therefore might not seek the praise or approval of others once the task is complete.

Just as greens don't like the restriction of organizing people on a task, they generally don't like being without options. Greens truly believe in the power of problem-solving and will not fret over potential future problems as they assume some kind of inventive solution can be found. However, if you limit the tools available to a green, problem-solving becomes more difficult. For example, when I pack for a trip, I don't worry all that much about what the weather will be like. Just knowing the season is good enough—I'll just pack enough clothing options that it won't matter. Similarly, I won't feel the need to plan out exactly what activities I'll do on the trip. I'll bring hiking boots to the beach just in case. As you can imagine, I prefer to drive rather than fly in these instances so that I'm not limited by an airline's idea of an "oversized" bag. I even get a little itchy when I have to ride somewhere with other people. "Now I have to really think about what time I have to leave and what I need to get back for," I'll think. "Now I have to plan." Having a getaway vehicle opens the possibilities of leaving whenever I need to and keeps my options open.

The Flip Side

Greens are often self-assured and confident of themselves. They have thought through their opinions thoroughly. They have a mental picture of success to which they judge their own performance without needing a lot of input from others. Greens generally don't mind being the odd man out in social settings. However, this self-assuredness can easily evolve into pride. Particularly when working in teams, greens need to be able to ask others for their opinions. While they feel comfortable judging their own success, they may be ignoring the wants or needs of others without realizing it. Simply asking for input, even when it doesn't feel necessary, will open greens up for improvement beyond what they can accomplish on their own. Greens need to be able to use their sense of objectivity to evaluate new information and new perspectives fairly. Further, the green who discusses their opinion or performance openly is forging relationships with other personality colors that are much needed.

Being literal and information-based can also easily lead greens to be insensitive to others. Simple questions like, "Do you like my new haircut?" to more complex questions like, "Why am I having these problems in my marriage?" when presented to a green can lead to a factual discussion of events and opinions that can be far too frank. However, if a green can become sensitive to others' feelings and remain tactful yet truthful, they can be a wellspring of honest but caring advice.

While greens can easily ignore some social norms, increasing their willingness to adhere to them may show their support for and desire for relationships with those around them. I remember being in a church service once when an announcement was made that an elder would be stepping down. The church was called upon to give recognition for his service, and everyone stood and clapped. My husband and I were new members, and when I didn't stand, my husband looked at me bewildered. "Why did you not stand?" he asked. "How can I recognize his service when I couldn't even recognize his face? I don't know him yet." If I had just gone along with the crowd, even if it didn't make complete sense to me at the moment, I would have sent a message of unity, gratitude, and a desire to be more integrated into the church body. While greens may see these social rules as unnecessary, they are still important for other personality colors. Make small talk, smile at people you don't know, take extra time to ask people about their lives, introduce yourself. Even if it doesn't feel natural, it can be an important message of solidarity to the rest of the team or church body.

Greens can easily go from seeming to be socially disconnected to actual isolation if they aren't careful. Greens need to recognize that they need people of other personality colors in their lives to provide the relationships, feedback, and support they need. While greens are unlikely to ask for help making decisions or for emotional support, they often realize their need for these things after they receive them. Greens, then, need to trust that they are better with relationships and place emphasis on fostering them.

Built Better With Green

While greens may often choose to work independently, they can also provide many strengths to social groups. However, this requires the commitment of the green person and the acceptance of the group. Identifying greens can help us better understand them and will allow their personality color to bring real benefits to group settings. Greens can be excellent mediators as they tend to be fair and impartial and weigh the information without allowing the relational or emotional aspects of the situation to sway their judgment. Greens are also good at giving advice. Greens don't feel as burdened by guilt as some others might while giving hard truths. Greens are also good at listening in a non-judgmental way as they receive confessions as information instead of having a strong emotional reaction. Greens are often good teachers as well since they enjoy accruing and relating information. Greens, and perhaps particularly green women, may feel out of place in church settings due to a justified emphasis on ministering to others with emotional warmth. Greens should be given a platform to use their unique skill sets and encouraged to contribute to the mission of the church.

Building With The Orange Personality

By Cindy Patton

"Mrs. Perry, we really need to work on Cindy staying in her seat and also her talking."

And with that sentence from my first-grade teacher at the first parent-teacher conference of the school year, my Mama cried all the way home. She had no idea there was anything "wrong" with my behavior at all. Mrs. M's comments made Mama feel as if she and Daddy were complete failures as parents in light of my six-year-old behavior having been critically assessed. I can now reflect on this situation using insights revealed by learning about personality colors. My teacher (as I recall from my insightful remembrances from my six-year-old mind!) was a stern, high gold, discipline-loving grandmother who expected her classroom to reflect as much. As a result, she was not quite as delighted with my free spirit as my family was.

Sitting Still Stifles

As an educator, I realize that orange children are often

required to behave at school in ways that are contrary to their wiring. We expect them to sit, often without moving or talking, for hours at a time. By the end of the day, they are literally ready to jump out of their skins—they just cannot "behave" that way. Sadly, our orange children can be mislabeled as disruptive (or as needing medication) when sometimes all they really need is the freedom to move. Educators recognize this as a kinesthetic learner—one who needs to have movement and interaction to best process and learn. These are our doers rather than our observers. Let them play through a new game to figure it out rather than reading the fourteen pages of rules!

Think about how school is structured: sit in your seat, raise your hand to speak, walk in a straight line, no talking in the halls, and sometimes even the dreaded silent lunch. Fellow oranges are beginning to hyperventilate, as am I, just reading this! This is completely opposite of the way oranges are wired. We need to move to process information, we tend to be blurter-outers instead of hand-raiser-uppers, we want to walk "in community" with our friends while chatting all the way—and eating, too, if possible!

Multiply this by twelve or thirteen years of a school setting, and one can get an insight as to how stifling this could be to our young oranges. These are not "bad kids." Many are just placed in often rigidly structured settings and expected to adhere to behavioral standards they cannot successfully maintain for hours, weeks, months, years on end, due to their wiring, not their abilities/inabilities.

We (the education field as well as society in general) need to combine pedagogies to accommodate all learning styles, including the outside-the-lines oranges. Of course, oranges need to be respectful of rules. We need to learn self-control. We need to stay in our seats and not be loud and disruptive. But I do think we can find a way to coexist within any environment so that all our personality colors can maximize our potential without compromising or inhibiting any others. We simply must recognize and validate that not everyone learns, processes, thinks, or reacts in the same way, even when we are all looking at the same situation. A "one size fits all" approach to educating, parenting, and even churching is a naïve (selfish?) approach that can cause confusion and misunderstanding at best and broken, damaged, often seemingly irreparable relationships at worst.

Beige Is Boring

As an orange, I need color and pattern to stimulate and inspire me in all parts of my life. My classroom reflected this. Even if you didn't know which classroom was mine, you would have been able to tell. When I first began teaching and was setting up my classroom with all the things that make me happy, a seasoned, non-orange teacher walked by and popped her head in. When she saw my room, her first statement to me was (in a whispery, low-toned voice), "Don't you think you might over-stimulate the children with all this?"

My response, which I'm sure was snippy/rude and a bit smart-alecky, was something along the lines of: "Since this is essentially my home for nine months of the year, I have to be motivated and stimulated, so NO, I do not think this will be over-stimulating to my students!" In my head, a curt "thank-you-very-much" was being played in a staccato rhythm!

Like most oranges, I am creative, a doodler, and dabble

in art—fun art, not fine art. This is the reason that I created my Nifty Notes for our speaking engagements and provided colored pencils at each table. I designed the Nifty Notes to reflect each personality color to go along with each of the color talks. These allow doodling and note-taking while engaging the brain just enough to not be distracted—perfect for all my oranges out there! We are fully aware that if left to our own orange devices, we can completely derail our own attention spans if we don't come up with a productive (NOT talking to everyone within earshot!), active way to stay engaged. What we are finding is that this method of notetaking is appealing to all the colors, not just to oranges. We strive to accommodate all colors in our presentations by creating an environment conducive to learning (and sometimes a gentle way to keep our oranges focused, on-task, and quiet!).

Free Spirit, Not Rule-Free

While I was a free-spirited, active child, I was also not allowed to be disrespectful. I was expected to obey my parents. I was expected to be well-behaved when at home or at friends' homes. I was expected to show respect and have manners ("Yes, ma'am," "No, sir..." I was reared in the South, you know!). Having an orange personality DID NOT mean I could just be out of control and rude.

Fellow oranges, we cannot ever use our wiring as an excuse to be irresponsible, rule-breakers, or just insensitive of others' feelings. Even now, I do not know how my parents navigated my childhood/teenhood in such a seemingly effortless way. The advantage I had was that my family appreciated and valued my sense of humor, spontaneity, energy, and "spunk!" These aspects of our personality can either be squelched or encouraged by our upbringing. Thankfully, mine were encouraged. Getting laughs for an orange is a means by which to receive acceptance and validation (our "love-language" if you will)!

I am keenly aware that all oranges do not find themselves living in such nurturing environments. Many grow up feeling the need to change or to be "fixed" (as if our methods and thought processes are somehow broken) or needing to please other "colors" in their close circle of acquaintances or loved ones. When we get together with friends and family, oranges love to be the center of attention or to at least have their presence acknowledged. This may be one reason why an orange will often not seek out another orange with whom to become friends. We tend to prefer being the "leading actor" on our own stages! Balancing our orange-ness with another color can create such a beautiful friend dynamic and benefit both individuals with strengths from the other. Instead of trying to make everyone else like me, embracing our differences results in a much stronger relationship. And we each must take honest and often hard introspective looks into our own weaknesses. No personality does everything well. We all have strengths and shortcomings that would benefit greatly when paired with the other personality types.

Did your parents follow the "everyone gets the same punishment" philosophy, or did they fall more toward the "equitable, not necessarily equal" camp? We can all reflect on our own upbringing and say, with honesty, "that worked, that didn't work, maybe this could have worked" as far as our own social, emotional, and spiritual training. And, fellow oranges, now might be a good time for all of us to whisper a collective prayer of gratitude for our parents, pleading forgiveness for our often rebellious/stubborn behaviors, and for our less than-precious mouths which, I'm sure got more than a couple of us in trouble. God knew that He did not wire us all the same; He is our Creator, and we are His Creatures.

Communication Is Critical

As an Army wife for the first nine years of our marriage, my orange personality served me well as my interactions and participation in activities were directly connected with my husband's jobs. It also was of great benefit that moving as often as we did those nine years were viewed more as adventures to me than as life-paralyzing occurrences. We would quickly seek out a new church home (I always loved that part). Then we would jump right in doing all the things involving our new church. I have always been the chatty, outgoing one (much kinder sounding than being labeled a loud-mouth). So, while I was "meeting and greeting" new people, Peter (not an orange) would often stand off to the side until I coerced him into conversations. I always tried to find connections back to Middle Tennessee, Lipscomb University, or the last Army post from which we had just moved. Oranges like to "connect the dots" with people; it makes us feel like we belong.

Early in our marriage, Peter stated one Sunday immediately after the worship service that he was going to the car to wait for me. When I eventually arrived at the car, I felt we needed to have a "discussion" (code: I was a little bit miffed at him!). I explained to him that my time of worship started after the concluding prayer. Interacting with people was what filled my spiritual tank. He, on the other hand, had experienced his worship via the singing, meditation, sermon, and Bible study. By the end of the service, he was satisfied—his tank was sufficiently filled. "Meeting and greeting" was not something he sought out or felt comfortable instigating himself. Once we were able to share how we each viewed our "church time," we were better able to make allowances (and extend grace) toward the other. One can see how these small differences of opinion could potentially cause some misperceptions, harsh words, and even some contentious views of the whole Sunday experience. He has never made me feel like I need to change who I am, how I do things, my outlook on life, or even how much I talk! As I say at every one of our speaking events, "Together, we make one really great person!"

There is another subject that could cause some real problems between an orange and a "non-orange" spouse...this is referred to in our house as "the B-word." Before any of you think the text just took a PG-13-rated turn, let me explain. I am referring to B-U-D-G-E-T; oft-times thought of in my mind like an ugly six-letter word! Because an orange, by nature, tends to be impulsive and not a lover of rules, a budget can feel restrictive and much too planned. In fact, that is a budget by definition. When the list-making, sensible spouse decides it's time "to sit down and go over every single one of our expenses for the week/month/year," don't be surprised if the orange in your life has retreated to another room in an eye-rolling, fetal position posture begging for it all to just STOP! While this may be a slight over-exaggeration, it still provides insight as to how an orange might not necessarily be the best person to appoint in making out the budget for the office, family, or (Heaven help us) church! This is NOT my spiritual gift. I own it, embrace it, and readily submit that task to any and all who feel that this is their calling. Knowing our weaknesses AND strengths allows each of us to embrace, utilize, and maximize our strengths and not apologize for our weaknesses.

Magnificent Or Mediocre

Most orange personality people I know have a creative side that is often seen in the performing, visual, culinary, or textile arts or in a variety of other avenues. However, one aspect that I feel every orange person shares is the feeling that their "work" could always be better, use a little improvement. What seems to be almost paradoxical rationale is truly how an orange thinks...we (you know, those "confident, enthusiastic orange people") need praise and recognition. Even writing that sentence rings notes of shallowness and neediness... and then I wonder if it's just me. But I hear it from other "known oranges" and realize that we are quite possibly the most seemingly confident people on the planet but crave and need affirmation. Yet non-orange people may think offering compliments, praise, or a sincere, "You did a good job," might be a catalyst for adding to our already "too much and she already knows she's good" personas. In reality, we need to hear it from our non-orange friends especially to show that we are capable of "reaching" an audience who may not think as we do.

We "think" what we did/created/made/performed was good, but is it really? I don't want to give the impression that the reason for this is just to be boastful or pompous, but it is literally what perpetuates and fuels continuing creativity for an orange. I may have an idea in my head for a piece of art, but until others see it and give me their feedback, I truly do not know if it's magnificent or mediocre. Many times, the end result is only vague in my mind's eye, and I don't even know until the very end what it will look like! This happens often with sewing, my collage art, and even at speaking engagements. Pre-planning for these can feel a bit restrictive so that leaves some rogue creativity going on... uncharted waters, so to speak. But the whispers of doubt run through my brain pointing out the flaws, mistakes, and imperfections. The voice in my head will always be quick to point out all the ways it could have been better.

While that orange exterior may look impervious to anything one could throw at it, just know that a well-placed, honest word of encouragement goes so very far with your orange acquaintances. They need to hear it from you.

I Wanna Win

"Please do not dare me to do something!" I've shared with friends before. Call it waving the red flag before the bull, if you will, but having a competitive spirit is part of an orange's make-up. Logic and awareness of one's limitations can sometimes be forfeited for the "I wanna win" mindset. Competitiveness can be seen in sports, in board games, or even where or how we spend our money (hello, the competitive concept "Keeping up with the Joneses."). Oftentimes, these displays can be witnessed by spectators or participants, but many times, the competition is only going on in the mind of the orange person. Permit me to explain.

After sustaining a serious injury and subsequent surgery, I required several weeks of physical therapy. My physical therapist recognized, after one of our first sessions, that one of the best ways to motivate me was in an almost "challenge" form. "I don't think you will be able to do this exercise" was my red flag. But a particular incident that stands out was a competition against my life-long nemesis: myself. The therapist needed me to do a timed exercise to see how many repetitions I could do within a certain time period. At the end of 30 seconds, she told me how many I had done. It wasn't good enough for me. Realizing what was going on, the therapist immediately said, "You want to do this again, don't you?" My opponent? The physically fit college athlete living in my mind's eye. No matter that I was now a sedentary-ish 60+-year-old grandmother forty years past the highlight reel that was running in my head. Maybe this offers some insights as to those weekend warrior injuries sustained by less-than-fit middle-aged men and women who still think they "have it." Yeah, we probably don't. We are competing with the eighteen-year-old versions of ourselves who really could. It's hard to acknowledge that another old foe, time, traipses on while we sometimes remain in a mental time-warp of athleticism, or simply, youth. Competing with time. Competing with the world. Competing with ourselves. "Winning" can be tiring.

The Flip Side

Oranges can have outgoing personalities, but those very traits can also be the impetus for some unwanted outcomes. Because oranges don't mind/love being the center of attention, this can sometimes result in a boastful, self-centered, "it's all about me" mentality. This mindset can even creep into something as noble as church or outreach ministries. We have seen this narrative before—a charismatic, charming spokesperson/leader takes the once honorable attention too far and finds him or herself in a compromised or even sinful situation. What once started with the best of intentions and motives implodes and has a negative consequence. Of course, this does not always happen, but oranges should certainly be aware of this possibility when finding themselves in roles of leadership.

Another trait that must honestly be broached is that an orange does not like conflict at all. In order to avoid conflict, an orange may choose to treat emotions or situations too flippantly or even exaggerate truths to maintain an "I want everyone to like me" persona. This does not endear an orange to others but instead perpetuates the idea that an orange just won't take things seriously and isn't always the most forthright and truthful.

While healthy (read that again oranges...H-E-A-L-T-H-Y) competition is natural and understandable, it can escalate to something that could possibly be damaging to families and individuals. Once our kiddos come along, we want our son/daughter to be the smartest, most athletic, best looking, kindest in all the land...and we now have placed our competitiveness upon the "performances" of our children. How tragic. Bragging rights for an orange are often thinly-disguised means by which to share with the world that "I am winning" at parenting, at finances/wealth, at fitness, at LIFE.

Oranges can have a tendency toward addictive personalities whether that manifests itself in pleasure, drugs/alcohol, adventure, or even social media. Knowledge of this may prevent an orange from starting down a road that is predisposed toward addictive tendencies. Of course, this is not true for all individuals with an orange personality; however, it is worth noting the possibility. Ancient writings said, "To know thyself is the beginning of wisdom."

Built Better With Orange

While one can sometimes become too focused on the negatives of any particular color, let me also point out that my orange-ness allows me to serve a unique role within the Living Color ministry and the work of our church. Oranges do not mind being in front of people...in fact, we love it. Because of this, I enjoy teaching our women's class and love it even more when I'm asked to speak at larger events and gatherings.

This is some people's worst nightmare or biggest fear but not for an orange! I do not mind being called upon at the last minute to lead a public prayer or to pray individually with someone. Meeting new people is exciting to an orange and does not cause us anxiety. Because we are wired by God in this way, there are natural places in the Kingdom where these very traits are not only valued but necessary. Need someone to meet new people when they come to church? Sign me up! Teacher unexpectedly can't make it to class? I'm your backup. Looking for someone to write and act in a skit and do all kinds of crazy? Pick me! Want someone to try some new idea knowing it may be a total bust? That's okay, too, because oranges do not mind making mistakes. It's just another way to re-think what didn't work and come up with a Plan B (or C or D or E. We are tenacious, that way!).

God has built into oranges a bit (okay, a lot!) of fearlessness which, when channeled properly, can have great and powerful Kingdom outcomes. Think of the positive impact having an orange on a mission team can have...the mission field is viewed as an adventure. Those lost souls who do not know a risen Christ? They are just friends we haven't met yet. Glass half-full outlook.

Oranges, it's very important to surround yourself with people who embrace (tolerate? inspire?) you as you are. The Living Color team knows me so well and makes me feel as if they would not change one thing about my personality. Do they "get" the way I do things all the time? Of course not. Do they value and seek my input when planning an event or conference? Absolutely. They have recognized that this impulsive, creative, loud, talkative, not-afraid-to-make-mistakes teammate has real value. I still make them a little nervous when I've not prepared for an event months/weeks/days in advance like some of them have. But they know that I will get it done because I have proven it in the past. Had I been negligent or tardy in my task, they would not have confidence in my methods, my abilities, or even in me.

It is vital that we oranges neither allow our strong personalities to completely run over and dominate others so that their "color-voice" is not heard nor make light of things so that we seem careless and irresponsible. There are times when some of these traits can be beneficial, but nobody, including other oranges, likes being around someone who is just too much ALL. THE. TIME. Reign it in, find the opportune and appropriate time, then orange like there's no tomorrow! We are made in HIS image—and HE delights in HIS creation!

Building With The Blue Personality

By Rhonda Beckham

It's 5:00 a.m., and my alarm goes off. I had knocked off early the night before because of a sinus problem and had taken NyQuil to help me sleep. As I hit the "stop" button on my phone to quiet the noise, I notice that I have missed two items during the night. The first is a text message at 12:30 a.m. that says, "Are you awake?" And the second is a missed call shortly afterward. Both are from Elizabeth, one of my girls from Bible class. My heart sinks immediately. I have told my girls over and over that I am available for them 24/7. If you need anything, call me. I will answer day or night. Now I've failed, I haven't been there when needed. It's one of the worst feelings I deal with—letting someone down. Welcome to being a blue.

Connection Is Key

As I learn more and more about what it is to be a blue, I realize I've seen threads of this color all through my life. I have a terrible memory. My mom always said that no one would notice if I developed Alzheimer's because I never could remember anything anyway. That being said, I have tried to remember the first time that I thought I was "different." I remember a time when I had written a creative writing piece in middle school. I had poured myself into the paper. It was a story about a girl who went through great obstacles because of some disease and ended up dying in the end (I know, terrible). As I watched my teacher read the words, I saw tears form in her eyes. She handed it back to me and told me it was beautiful. Something was ignited in my brain with a feeling that I had connected with her. I had connected my thoughts with hers and caused an emotion. She had looked into my thoughts and found me worthy of feeling something. Connecting is imperative for a blue.

I have sought this connection all my life: from family, friends, co-workers, students, parents, colleagues—anyone that I come in contact with. It starts out simple with the person across the counter at the grocery store. "How's your day? Have you tried the caramel-covered popcorn? (my Achilles heel) I heard it's addictive." There are very few people or dogs that I will not try to talk to and quite possibly hug. Blues love to hug. For example, through my gold friend Debbie's conversations about her friend Ramona, I felt like I knew Ramona and loved so many things I had heard about her. One day, I saw Ramona at McDonald's and immediately spread my arms to say hello. I felt connected to her without her even knowing who I was. She, being a green, was a little wide-eyed and apprehensive (to say the least) of my approach because we had never properly met. I had come on too strong, and I learned quite a bit that day. Not everyone shares my enthusiasm for hugging. Some people like to be asked so they can say, "No, thank you." A blue, however, thinks a good strong hug is a great way to communicate a warm welcome, even with a stranger. But it doesn't have to be a hug: a smile is a connection to me, and I claim victory when I get one in return. This need for connection is more complex than just a temporary response. Connectivity blossoms into relationships, and blues crave relationships.

Rollercoaster Of Relationships

Relationships can make or break a blue. A relationship that's a safe haven for a blue to be themselves is the best feeling ever. Good friends will catch you crying during a sad movie, or let's be honest, a happy movie. They may even make a joke about it, but you know they love you to pieces because you have such a big heart. These friends know they will never shed a tear that you are not going to match because you feel their sadness—at times, maybe more than you are supposed to, but we'll get to that later. I hate to see someone cry alone; I will always oblige. And it is not just sadness. I will match your joy as well. The crying is just an easier identifier. As a blue, I love to roll around in the good feeling of being loved. It is the feeling you have when you wrap your favorite blanket around your shoulders and curl up on the couch, and boy, do I love that feeling. It's the feeling of being accepted. Laughter comes easy, and everything is peaches and cream, sunshine, and roses. Then let conflict raise its ugly head, and the blue will immediately retreat. Conflict is a blue's worst nightmare.

Conflict Is A Killer

Blues see conflict as a killer to relationships. There is a risk of losing your connection to one or both of the parties involved. I want to be Switzerland, and that is not always possible. You love them all so much; you want everyone to be happy. After all, that is a blue's paradise! We are "conflict-dodgers," and tension is the forerunner to conflict. Tension to a blue is exaggerated because we anticipate and dread the moment when we will be pulled into the conflict and have to "pick a side." No longer will we be able to hide out and avoid it. The first gray I noticed in my hair came during a time of conflict at church. The tension seemed to be mounting week after week, and I was waiting for the reckoning—the time when I would no longer be able to sit on the sidelines and observe. While pulling my hair back into a ponytail, I noticed two gray stripes coming up the back of my neck. *Gray*—against my dark brown hair! I had tried to suppress the anxiety that came with walking through the doors of the church, and it had released itself in the form of a skunk on the back of my head!

The most difficult times in my life trying to maintain neutrality and restore peace have likely been when raising teenagers. You know how it is, little conflicts that arise between your kids and your husband, or big ones. I remember a time when my daughter wanted to attend a weekend event, and my husband had said no. I love them both and understood both sides. Because I could sympathize with both, I played the fence, consoling each one when they weren't together. But there came a time when I had to face the music and get right in the middle of it.

Being in the middle taught me several things. First of all, honesty with both parties is so important. A blue will try to placate each side to avoid disappointing anyone. Therefore, being completely honest is a challenge because of fear of rejection. If you are honest from the beginning, it will save heartache in the end. In the situation above, I played both sides. I agreed with each side when they talked to me about it. I should have thought about the issue and taken a stand, not about how to maintain peace. Of course, taking a stand as a blue is not waving a banner and putting my marching boots on. It is saying things like, "I understand what you are saying, and I am sorry that you are hurting, but you need to look at this from your dad's point of view. You know he loves you and wants what is best for you. Part of that love is doing what he thinks is best, and that's what's happening here." Hug inserted here, of course.

Second, people will respect you more if you speak truth to them. The Bible calls it "speaking the truth in love." Sometimes it may be difficult to know where a blue truly stands because they are trying to maintain peace. By constantly dodging how you really think, you can cause people to lose respect for you. They will always think, "Does she really think that, or is she agreeing with me?" Be confident in your relationships, and trust that true friends will love you for being honest with them. Someone that just wants a "girl, you are so right!" all the time isn't a true friend.

Unmet Expectations

Blues are dreamers or maybe I should say movie producers. Take any future plans: a blue will produce a movie in her head about how that event will go. For example, I bought tickets to a Beth Moore conference that would happen in about nine months. I started the script: "Hot diggity dog, this is going to be sooooooo much fun! My daughter and daughter-in-law will come with me. We will have the most amazing road trip to Woodstock, Georgia. Singing NEEDTOBREATHE, Lauren Daigle, and Elevation Worship at the top of our lungs. Gut-busting laughter. Intense, deep conversations. Luxurious hotel. Dining experiences to brag about for months. And Beth—need I say more?! Spiritual bonding is the best!!! The three of us will be forever connected by this experience. We will …" and on and on and on I go. Sounds like fun, right? The problem comes when the reality is different from my movie, as was the case here. My sweet girls were not able to go. I was deflated. I'm ashamed to say that it affected me for more than a few days. A blue can feel the loss of something that never happened. I must, as a blue, constantly remind myself of what is real and what I have cooked up in my head.

By keeping the movies to a minimum, blues will avoid disappointment and will not miss the joy of the unexpected. In the situation above, I tried to sell my tickets, with no luck. My son Taylor encouraged me to go by myself. WHAT?! ALONE?! I put on my big girl panties and hit the road. I called my husband upon arriving at the luxurious hotel and then turned my phone off. I sat on the bed with an open Bible to Psalms and had a wonderful time with God's word. The next morning there was only one person to worry about—myself. I got to the church early and went to center stage, the third row, because it is easy to find that kind of seat for just one. During worship time I didn't care what others around me thought because I didn't know them—I lifted my hands high in response to the words, just me and God. And then Beth took the stage, and do you know what? She started in the book of Psalms– the very passage I had studied the night before in the luxurious hotel! GOD WANTS TO BLESS YOU… allow Him room to work His wonders.

Falling Short Spirals Into Falling Flat

Blues do not want to disappoint. The feeling of disappointing someone is an absolute gut-punch to me. I believe that if you ask me to do something, you have already thought it through and decided that I should be able to do it (otherwise you wouldn't have asked). If I say no, I will disappoint you. That's how I think, rational or not. It is a blue's perspective, and therefore a blue's reality. When I was a kid, my father never spanked me (yes, those were the days of a good ole paddling). He never had to. He could give me a look—you know the one, the one of disappointment. It cut into my soul. It still does today.

I can carry the guilt of letting someone down like a cloud over my head. It can quickly spiral from feeling like a disappointment to just one person to feeling like just a disappointment. If I was supposed to call someone during the week, but it slipped my mind, the minute I see them I panic and worry about what they are going to think of me. Again, my mind runs away with me, and I imagine what they must have thought day after day. "What a loser she is. I was really counting on her, and she didn't come through. She isn't dependable. She isn't reliable. She won't get a second chance from me!" This imaginary conversation erupts in a few seconds, and I'm apprehensive about contact. Many times, as it turns out, the one that I have slighted doesn't even remember. To them, it was no big deal, but I've gone through the emotions and am exhausted.

As a blue, my need to connect with and love others leads to a feeling of real responsibility for them. I'm constantly thinking of how to make others feel loved. I have great intentions. I will hear of a need, make a mental note to myself to offer assistance, and sometimes even put it on a post-it note in my calendar. On a typical day, if I am at school or church, I make about thirty to forty of these mental notes, depending on how many people I have conversations with. There is no way that I will be able to fulfill all the beautiful and meaningful acts of kindness that I thought would show my concern for them, but I feel the disappointment of not doing ALL of the things I set out to do. I can beat myself up for not showing love as I should.

Let me give you an example I had recently. I have been on the receiving side of so many acts of love and kindness because I have recently battled breast cancer. My dear friend Paula reached out to me to have lunch, and I was so glad to get to spend time with her. Her first words to me were, "I am so sorry for being such a horrible friend." It shocked me to hear her say such a thing. When I asked her why she felt this way, she showed her blueness. She had "intended" to do so much more for me during my recovery and didn't follow through with those intentions. Of course, I had no idea of these unmet self-expectations, but I immediately knew the feeling she was having. As mentioned before, she probably had produced a movie in her mind of how it would play out, the oohs, the hugs, the tears of joy…and then she destroyed the whole thing by not following through. Even though I didn't see the movie, I had written that script a thousand times. This guilt can keep a blue from reaching out to someone because they think the other person sees them as a "horrible friend." The guilt that a blue will feel because they haven't acted on these intentions is paralyzing.

Spreading Sunshine

To overcome this feeling of guilt, blues need to keep it simple. Act on what you can do and not what you think you should do. Curb the urge to "make a big gesture" to express just how much you care. Sending a quick text that says "You were on my mind this morning, and I hope you have a wonderful day" is showing love. It shows encouragement, which is one of blue's greatest strengths. Even if you don't get this small act accomplished, show yourself grace and don't get bogged down in the guilt of unmet self-expectation. The reality is that no one knows except you—forgive yourself.

One of the best examples I have seen of keeping it simple but effective is from a former student of mine, Kallie. At the time, she was new to our small school and painfully shy. Although she barely spoke a word, her ability to encourage and lift people up was uncanny. In her quiet way, she observes people, me included. If I had a bad day, I would find a note on my desk that afternoon from Kallie. It could be as simple as a post-it note with just the words "I love you." Sometimes it was a finished page from a coloring book that she had signed—along with a heart. Sometimes it was a letter that lifted my spirits, with an encouraging word, an "I love you," and ALWAYS a verse. At the beginning of this year, she wrote a letter, praying blessings on the year ahead. Along with the letter were envelopes entitled "Open When." They were for days when I would be stressed, when I needed a laugh, or when I needed prayer. It was an arsenal of encouragement—from someone who barely talks. When I talked to her dad about her gift for encouragement, he told me that she has, behind her door, a prayer wall. He said he recognized some names on the wall as family, friends, and teachers but asked who this or that person was. She replied that it was someone she heard of at school, and they needed prayers. That person will never know that sweet Kallie had lifted them up to the Father, but isn't that the very best way to show love?

The Flip Side

Although characterized by their outpouring of love for others, blues can be self-focused. The constant worry about what others think about us can make us spiral into despair. Analyzing the words and actions of everyone is based on one thing: how it affects me.

One snare for a blue is becoming consumed with the actual task instead of the outcome. Let me explain. Ironically, there is a deep need for a blue to be needed. The satisfaction from being asked to fill a role of comforter in someone's grief/need/sickness/drama, etc. is like a drug to the blue. We cannot get enough. It can turn into something unhealthy. Several years ago, my friend's mother was very ill. Being a "good friend," I was at her side as her mother's health was declining. I would go to the hospital, run errands, get food, chat it up with visitors, get to know the siblings and their kids. I felt like I became part of their family, and I LOVED it. It became a haven for me. I felt as if I belonged, and I was helping with whatever need they had. The family accepted me and never made me feel uncomfortable about how much time I spent with them or how intrusive I probably was. In hindsight, I realize that I crossed into a situation that wasn't healthy for this blue and was not what they needed at such a time. In fact, it evolved into pride on my part. In my mind, no one could "fill in the blank" like me. No one could love them better than me. No one showed concern for them like I did. No one had the inside information like I did. I was the right person to do all these things because this blue girl was the best at loving, helping, doing, caring, etc. This situation became my world, my problem, my sadness. After her mother passed, I was at a loss. Sure, I felt the loss of someone, but more deeply, I felt the loss of something. What would I do now that there was no need? The task had become more than the outcome. I had lost sight of being there for my friend because I needed comforting myself!

Another snare, if not careful, is that blues can play the victim card like a champ. It is a temptation to become the "poor, pitiful me" because people will hug you, say nice things, encourage you, etc. Sometimes, we will present our situation in the worst possible light, exaggerating the details to gain sympathy. We feel the outpouring of love come our way, and it feels good. My daughter and her fiancé decided to elope to Colorado and get married—just the two of them. A date was set, and plans were made. Once they decided to go this route, it seemed as if a load had been lifted off their shoulders. Truly, I could not have been happier for both of them and truly, I was okay with it. But here's what happened. When I told people of their plans, inevitably I would be asked, "You aren't going? Are you okay with that?" I found myself answering, "No, we aren't going (with a face). It's okay (insert slight shrug here)." WHAT ARE YOU DOING, RHONDA?! My feeling turned from "everything is so great" to "yes, I'm being strong in this trying time. Please hug me." I made it about me. I traded the confidence and happiness that I have for my daughter for a momentary feeling of sympathy for myself. That, my friend, is pride. Blues need to be keenly aware of keeping it 100. No need for manipulation.

Built Better With Blue

There you have it. My blue self in a short synopsis. I can honestly say that I haven't always loved myself. Part of that is because I didn't understand why I think and react the way I do. I thought of myself as weak. I looked at others and thought, "Why can't I be like them, so bold, so confident, so sure of themselves, so organized, so productive....." and on and on. That is what we blues do, compare. It is when I quit comparing myself to others and prayed for insight into who God made ME to be that I have found peace and contentment. What I have found through the Living Color Conferences after my talk is voices that say, "Me too." It is validation, and it is a beautiful, enlightening event. It is learning that I can approach my best self by living and working through my color and not around it and certainly not trying to be something I am not. I find encouragement to stop comparing and start working together to do Kingdom work. And when I fall into that comparison trap of Satan, I remind myself that this blue is fearfully and wonderfully made by the Creator.

Building With The Gold Personality

By Debbie Mankin

I began my career as a guidance counselor at a small Christian school with grand ideas of how I was going to make everything run smoothly using my gold personality to its fullest advantage. At the time, it was the job of the guidance counselor to get grades on paper copies from all the teachers in seventh through twelfth grades and then enter them into the computer program that would then put them on report cards (yes, I know we were still in the Dark Ages back then). Weeks in advance, I would let the teachers know when they needed to turn their grades in to me, thinking that I had given them plenty of time to do what was needed to have their grades ready. And invariably, there would be teachers who never got me the grades on time. When I complained to my principal who was one of the wisest men I ever met and also gold like me, he told me, "Now, Debbie, you have to remember that everyone is not like you!" That statement still resonates in my mind when I expect people to do things like I want them done. Making sure things are done on time in an orderly manner is an integral part of my gold personality. Not everyone is gold, but it often helps to have a gold personality assisting a group to accomplish the group goals. I soon learned that working on report cards would always be long days for me as I made sure that all grades were eventually turned in and accurately reported.

Love A List

Do you keep a list and check off the accomplishments as you complete them? This trait defines someone with a gold personality. I have always made lists and thought most of my life that everyone else did too. If my list was not on paper, I could carry it around with me in my head.

I bought a little notebook when I first became the guidance counselor at my school and kept a running list of what I intended to accomplish during the day and even for the week. It gave me great satisfaction to be able to put a checkmark beside something on my list. One of the things that I learned early on as the guidance counselor was that the structured day that I had had as a teacher in a classroom did not always work the same way in the guidance office. My list of what I wanted to accomplish in a day would often have to go by the wayside when a student or parent or even a teacher showed up on my doorstep needing my assistance. It caused me great consternation until I finally told myself that the first thing on my list needed to be helping others. The other things on my list had to come second. My job got better when I finally came to that realization.

One of the first things that I did at the beginning of my retirement was to make a list of all the things that I hoped to accomplish in the next few years. I was delighted to list projects that I had wanted to do for years but never seemed to have time to start and finish. I am now into the second year of retirement and have not done much on that list yet. I pull out the list every now and then just to remind myself what I wrote so I can look forward to checking something off! It will happen with time, and I will feel a great sense of accomplishment. Golds feel a sense of urgency once something goes on a list, whether it is a mental or physical list. If someone with a gold personality is taking on a big project that requires multiple items on a list, it is like a burden has been placed on his or her shoulders until that responsibility is completely done. Golds even feel the burden if they are working on a group project because they have formulated in their minds the results and feel that they must "oversee" what everyone else is doing to make it come out "just right." This can come across as pushy if you do not understand gold. Golds must remind themselves that others do not always see the world the same way they do.

Crave Control

Do you always like to be in control? Those with a strong gold personality have a strong sense of order, and therefore, they feel that things need to be done a certain way. They expect others to know and meet their expectations. If someone decides that the gold standard is not always needed, then the gold person may struggle to not demand his or her way.

This was demonstrated when my gold friend, Eric Goslowsky, began teaching Army Junior Reserve Officers' Training Corps (JROTC) for a local high school in Franklin,

Tennessee, after retiring as a colonel from an Army career. He is in charge of approximately 160 students, and he began his career as a teacher hoping that he would be in charge of a disciplined group of kids who were yearning for a career in the military or hoping to attend a military service school. He did not find this to be true with the majority of his students. His "goldness" really came to light when he was working with one of his young senior officers. This is his story in his words.

"On Tuesday every week, we require the JROTC uniform to be worn. This implies a complete ensemble with a dress coat and beret. After the last bell had rung one Tuesday, I went outside to help direct traffic. While at the crosswalk, one of my more senior JROTC officers walked by holding her entire uniform draped over her arm but wearing her black dress shoes. Of course, every gold button in my body was pressed at the same time! I looked down at her shoes and then looked up at the cadet and said, 'Seriously?' Gleefully, smiling like a Cheshire cat, she said, 'I didn't bring any other shoes and what did it matter?' What did it matter! It went against every organized, directed, structured, and focused thought in my brain! Apparently, my disappointment showed in my face as I grimaced and rolled my eyes. Knowing that I could not control the situation worried me more than the actual infraction. It was minutes later that the same student sent me a message stating how sorry she was for being out of uniform but, more importantly, how insensitive she felt for my feelings being a career military officer. She knew the uniform, and what it represented, meant more to me than she remembered."

The gold personality holds fast to traditions and has a hard time when someone does not abide by them. Their sense of control is violated when someone decides to step away from traditions that they have tried to instill in others. Family is very important to golds because of those traditional values. Biological families hold a special place in the heart of a gold, but team members can be thought of like family when they buy into what the gold holds important.

Fight For Fairness

Have you always been a rule follower? If so, you likely have a strong sense of justice, especially for those who do not follow the rules. Whenever a gold person is faced with a situation where someone has been treated unfairly, then the gold makes it his or her responsibility to rectify the problem if possible.

I worked at a non-profit organization where I oversaw pairing adult learners with tutors to help them with literacy skills. I paired myself with a young woman who wanted to get her GED. She had two little girls and was expecting a third daughter. We worked together for months for her to be able to study and pass the tests to obtain her high school diploma. She and I became friends in the process.

One day she called me to tell me that she had bought a used car in a nearby city and that it had started giving her trouble even before she got back home. She had called the dealership for several days to try and return the car and was getting the runaround about what she could do. I pictured her broken down on the side of the road with her three girls in the car with her. She had put a large down payment on the car and set up monthly payments at an exorbitant rate. She did not know how to navigate the whole situation, and the salesman had taken advantage of her.

I told her that I would meet her and drive back to the dealership with her to see if I could help. While we drove, I asked her to let me do the talking when we arrived, and I spent the next thirty minutes praying for the Lord to give me the words to say. She and I walked into the dealership and found just the owner there when we arrived. I explained to him that as the mother of three small children she had to have a reliable car and that the one she had purchased was not. He offered to fix it, but I insisted that she just needed to return the car at this point. We discussed the down payment, and I told him that he could keep a small portion of the money since she had had the car for several days. I asked that he return the rest to her. To my amazement, he pulled out a wad of bills from his pocket and counted out the money to her. I then asked that they both sign the original paperwork that said she would make monthly payments after I added a statement that she had returned the car and would not owe any money. He did what I asked after a lengthy discussion.

We walked out of the dealership feeling that she had been treated fairly. She later found a good used car with my help and made a much more reasonable purchase agreement before buying it. I felt like justice had triumphed in the end, a feeling that all golds strive to achieve.

Always Asserting Advice

Are you always ready to give others your opinion of how things should be done? Then your gold side is shining. When my first grandson was born, I was the proudest grandmother out there you could find. Since he was the first child of my oldest son, I had years of advice stored up just ready to give my son now that he was taking care of one of my most precious gifts from God. I had done a good job of raising him (at least in my eyes), so I knew that he was just waiting to hear my vast wisdom on what he needed to be doing with his new son. It did not take many times of me spewing advice to him on what he should and should not be doing before he let me know that he and my daughter-in-law had to figure this all out by themselves. They have done a great job of raising this child without daily advice from me. My new grandson brought me a new viewpoint on how a gold needs to handle advice-giving.

Gold personalities are ready and waiting to hand out their advice on any and every subject. One of the best compliments that I was ever given from a green friend of mine was that you need to listen when golds tell you something because they usually know what they are talking about. However, that does not mean that all those with a gold personality need to go around telling everyone in earshot what to do. Golds must learn to wait until they are asked before they tell others what needs to be done. That is not always easy since golds are always planning in their heads how things need to go. However, if advice is needed, then others should consider seeking out a gold if they know that the gold knows to wait to be asked and does not just offer up suggestions at will. Golds also must learn to not take it personally if all their advice is not heeded. Just because advice may be sought does not mean that it must be followed, only considered.

Trustworthy But Only Tolerable

Are you known for being the dependable one in a group?

Golds are known for getting things done. If you give a gold something to do, then you do not have to worry that it will not happen. Golds can be counted on to take care of details that others may not even consider. One of the women at our church, Mary Dee Francis, is known far and wide for being the one to call on for any event that involves food. She can plan a meal, decorate for the occasion, and clean up in the blink of an eye. Overseeing food preparation has truly become her ministry. I know when I ask her to take care of the food for our conferences that I do not have to give it another thought. It comes across as effortless to those who are not gold. But as a fellow gold, I know the time and thought that she puts into making every occasion special that she coordinates and making sure all the details are handled.

Golds know that they are trustworthy, but they can also feel that they are only tolerated by others for the jobs that they can do. Golds are generally not the life of the party or the one hugging everyone as they come through the door or the one rattling off the research on the latest idea. Their sensible side makes them stay grounded to accomplishing the tasks at hand, but this can also make them feel like others do not really want them around because they are always handing out orders. In my younger days, I worried that being the gold person that God had called me to be was not endearing me to other people. When I "allowed" myself to show the world who I was while seeking only the approval of God, then my gold light shined brighter. Do not get me wrong—golds can be annoying when accomplishing goals, but the other colors can learn to appreciate the benefit of having a gold on their team.

Spend Time And Money Sensibly

Is being frugal with your money as well as your time just what you do? Being efficient with time is part of why planning is so important to those with a gold personality so that they accomplish the most in the least amount of time. However, frugality with money is a close second to time management.

This was demonstrated well when my gold friend, Nancy, started a ladies' ministry program at our church. She carefully thought out how much money she would need in the budget for the different activities that she had planned for the ladies. She was careful to do thorough research before spending any money to make sure that she was getting the best value for each dollar she spent. She was able to put together a wonderful women's conference for almost 200 women the first year without spending much money.

When Nancy had to step aside for a short period of time to handle some family matters, two of us on her planning team stepped in to assist with a new budget for the next year. When we approached the church treasurer to inquire how much Nancy had spent that year, he told us that she had allotted money for a conference but had not used it yet. She had been so frugal with her budget that he did not even realize that she had paid for the whole conference and barely made a dent in the budget. At the end of the year, there was enough money left in her budget that we were able to make a generous donation to a very worthy cause and still stay under the budget amounts that Nancy had established.

I was taught that being frugal can become a prideful thing if not handled carefully. I learned how to stretch the money as was needed early on in my marriage. God had to show me that He was really in control of my money, not me, when my husband lost his job. I had left my teaching job, and I was running a small business out of my home in order to stay home with my first child. It did not bring in a lot of money, but while my husband was looking for another job, it provided what we needed to pay our bills and get by. God provided me with plenty of customers during that time, and we never had to touch our savings. I was thankful that I knew how to be frugal, but I truly learned to appreciate that it is always God who blesses me with the money and material possessions that I need.

You do not have to worry that a gold person is going to go on a spending spree, especially when it is someone else's money being spent. Each financial decision is well thought out. If you want to stretch a dollar, just ask a gold how to do it. If you want to use your time efficiently, ask a gold for advice.

The Flip Side

Do these traits mentioned describe how you approach your life? People with gold personalities make the world function in a way so that details are taken care of and order is maintained. But golds can come across as too demanding to the other colors if they do not take care to understand that their need for organization does not always motivate the other colors. This characteristic of a gold appears bossy to others. When we first presented one of our color workshops, one of the gold mothers learned traits about her orange daughter that she had never realized. She also figured out that she had imposed her "goldness" on her daughter while she raised her and did not always allow her orange daughter to be the person that God had gifted her to be. In tears, she stood before the group and apologized publicly to her grown daughter for what she had done. This gold mother was able to pull off any project that she was given, but she learned from our workshop that other colors bring something to this world that we all need.

Golds can become so intent on checking off their lists that they forget to put people first. Accomplishing the tasks on their list is so imperative that they can make others feel that they are not important enough to take time for them. Golds often struggle to ask for forgiveness when they offend someone because they understand their motives and assume others do also. It is a big deal when someone with a gold personality says the words, "I'm sorry." Sometimes they have to be reminded that it is needed to show compassion. However, care must be taken that the long explanation given by a gold as to why the actions were taken is not the gold's way of asking for forgiveness. It is just pushing the control button.

The need for control in all situations can push a gold to anger if that control seems out of reach or not understood. I have reacted in a situation resulting in my temper flaring because things are not going the way I think they should be. It is not a pretty sight. Golds want to "fix" everyone else's problems to ensure that they are in control. This response is done out of love, but it can be perceived as interfering. I have learned to stop and try to put myself in the shoes of the other person who may not see the situation the same as me. Golds need to cultivate that trait.

Gold personalities must be careful to not let their need for order and structure turn into an obsessive compulsion. It is easy to pick out the gold person in a work setting by looking at that person's desk or simply by walking into his or her home. There is a place for everything, and everything needs to be in the right place for them to function well. But this tendency can carry over to golds expecting everyone else around them to perform in the same manner. Golds need to recognize that their need for perfection may not be the same standard that greens, oranges, and blues require. And they must learn to accept the ways others see and function in the world without judging them, even if they are not the same as gold.

Built Better With Gold

Daniel Pink, in his book, *When—The Scientific Secrets of Perfect Timing,* describes how groups function best. He says, "Group timing requires a boss—someone or something above and apart from the group itself to set the pace, maintain the standards, and focus the collective mind."[1] The Living Color team allows me to be the person that God has called me to be using my high gold characteristics. They give me permission to organize our team and allow me to coordinate all the information that must be communicated to set up a conference. They trust me to work out the details, and I trust them to contribute to the team in the ways that God has gifted them. It makes what I do more enjoyable because they allow my nature to direct to be used to accomplish our purposes. I know this would not work if they did not understand me. And because they do understand me, I try not to let my organizational skills overwhelm them. We recognize that when we come together as a team that God gifts us through his Holy Spirit to come up with ideas that would not happen if we approached our decisions as individuals. We hope to teach everyone that when all the colors work together as a team, wonderful things happen. God knew what He was doing when He created each of our unique personalities.

Renovating Our Self Perception

Debbie's grandkids, who are six and ten years old, recently purchased an incredibly hard 1000-piece Disney puzzle in the shape of Mickey's head. They had it spread out on their dining room table to complete it. Debbie's granddaughter asked her if she would like to help with it, and she eagerly accepted the invitation. Debbie was informed that they had already separated the pieces according to colors to make it easier to put the whole puzzle together. These children had already figured out how to make hard things easier. Bringing together all the colors was how they were able to see the big picture. All of us on the Living Color team hope that you come to understand that seeing all the personality colors as they apply to our lives makes it easier to understand how they fit together to make the big picture of God's kingdom. Here is what we hope you have learned about each color after reading the four color chapters:

- A green personality is associated with someone who is known for being analytical and who loves research and information. Greens are prone to take a long time to make a decision because they want to weigh every option. They prefer to work alone and dislike emotional expression, especially physical touch except with a few they know well. They are not intuitive. With their creative and visionary insight, they can come up with ingenious ways of solving problems given time.

- An orange personality is associated with someone who loves to have fun and enjoys being surrounded by people. They love to move and talk and are stimulated by their environments. Following the rules is not always important to them if they can achieve their goals. They can be impulsive especially when spending money, and they enjoy spontaneity. Their creative side allows them to think outside of the box. This may result in a struggle to appreciate their own work. Their competitive nature pushes them in all aspects of their lives.
- A blue personality is associated with someone who holds relationships with others in high regard. Connection to others is essential, and they love to hug. They cannot tolerate conflict and will avoid it if possible. They envision their lives as a movie in their heads with a happy ending of their making. They never want to disappoint. Loved ones (including pets) are their priority and are shown love with simple gestures. Being accepted is what they value.
- A gold personality is associated with someone who sees organization as an important part of life. Golds think that a list is the first step in undertaking their goals and love to check off each accomplishment. They like to be in control of all situations and enjoy being able to "fix" a problem. Rules are important to them

because they think that when everyone follows the rules, fair treatment results. They love to give out advice, are dependable, and can be trusted to take care of any project. They value frugality with money and time.

Empowerment Examples

Bob Goff in his book, *Everybody Always,* said, "Here's the deal: when we act like someone we're not, it's often because we're not happy with who we are. We might think we need other people's permission or love or approval before we can live our lives and pursue our beautiful ambitions. It's both good and bad. It's good if it causes us to want to pursue Jesus' love and approval more. But it's bad if we miss out on who God uniquely made us to be so we can be who someone else thinks we should be. God has never looked in your mirror or mine and wished He saw someone else."[2]

Our goal in conducting our conferences is to show you how to embrace your color so that you can apply the strengths and overcome the weaknesses to work in the Kingdom. Through our personal experiences and from our conferences, we have witnessed the validation and embracing of empowerment for those who come to understand their color.

Groundbreaking Green

Because greens are sometimes so reserved, it may not be obvious that they have committed to a group. Sara, a green, grew up with a group of similarly aged girls in her church's youth group. As they got older, the group noticed that Sara often didn't reply to text chains and when she arrived at events,

Sara didn't engage in the conversations as much. Fearing that they had grown apart, the group asked Sara if she still enjoyed being in the group. Sara was surprised and commented that she thought of them as her best friends. The revelation of identifying a green personality often helps both the green person and the people around the green person to understand their behavior. As the green presenter at Living Color Conferences, I have heard from many people who identify green personalities in their lives that knowing their personality color provides a new lens through which to view the person.

Outstanding Orange

As the orange presenter on our Color team, I was looking forward to meeting Michelle, who I suspected was orange. She met us at the venue where the conference was scheduled for the following day, and I immediately picked up on her orange-ness! Bubbly and outgoing, she came into the parking lot on two wheels, eager to meet the team. We walked inside to a beautifully decorated and colorful hall where she proceeded to excitedly share with us all the little details that she had included—and all the colors! It was perfect!

The next morning at the conference, I sensed a lack of appreciation (and possibly an air of dismissal?) for Michelle/orange, a leader at this congregation. I realized we needed to establish credibility and give some insights for her and other oranges. I suspected that she was an orange conforming to a gold role.

As I stood to speak, I made sure to make a mental note of where Michelle was sitting. Our team very much relies on body language and other non-verbal cues to help us get a "read" of our audience throughout our presentations. The more I shared my story, the more Michelle nodded in agreement. Further into my presentation, though, I noticed Michelle's head drop; looking back up, tears were flowing. I was describing her to an audience who, to this point, may not have fully appreciated her role or her orange ways. Details from my life and the way I (and many oranges, I dare say) have felt or been treated, were touching places in her heart that she, too, had experienced. Seeing her tears fueled me even more because I was able to speak specifically about her gifts and how the church there was SO blessed to have her talent and personality there. I called her by name. I praised her planning and set-up of our venue. I encouraged her to keep on with her orange self in doing a job that can often be more criticized than applauded. And I simply tried to educate our audience that even though Michelle/oranges may not do things the way they think they should be done, she was able to bring such a unique and personal perspective to their ministry.

After my part of the presentation, Michelle came up to me and thanked me for telling my/HER story. She said it was so wonderful to hear another person whose "wiring" was like hers and how that personality was an integral part of Kingdom-work. Notice—it is a PART of Kingdomwork. When all our colors appreciate each other, work within our strengths, and work with each other, we are much better equipped to reach others for King Jesus!

Beautifully Blue

One of the "revelations" from the conferences for me as the blue presenter was at one of our Living Color Conferences.

After our color talks, I had two young ladies come to me. Both were teachers, and both were very blue. What they learned through my talk was that blues will avoid conflict at all costs, sometimes avoiding it when it most certainly needs to be addressed. Both told me that they hated to send emails to parents about students who were becoming a problem. I could certainly relate to this being a teacher myself. They said that they will avoid sending any kind of negative information to the parent about their child until it gets out of hand. When they finally send the "We've got a big problem with little Jimmy" letter, parents are shocked—because they thought everything was going so smoothly—because as a blue the teachers didn't want to rock the boat.

Being honest is always the best way to go for a blue even when it is difficult. Blues need to address problems early, before they get out of hand. Go ahead and write that email; be honest and straightforward. Difficult for a blue, but it MUST be done.

Genuine Gold

We as the presenters leave our conferences hoping we have made a difference in the lives of those who hear our presentation. As the gold presenter, I was so surprised to receive an email from a woman in charge of organizing the upcoming color conference at her church. I had met Johnie the first time when we presented at her church only a few weeks earlier. As the gold person on our color team, it is my job to organize all the details of each conference with someone from the church before we go. I had worked with another woman for our first conference at that church. The material that we presented at the first conference had been so well received that we had been asked to return to bring them some more information about how the colors worked together.

Johnie had sat near the back at that first conference as each of us got up to do our presentations. As I always do, I had noticed her as I scanned the room as the other color presenters were talking. I like to try and figure out what color the participants are just by their reactions as each color is explained. I was not sure what color Johnie was until she showed up in my gold group when we broke into color groups for one of our activities. She opened up in that group and shared some of her past gold experiences with everyone.

When I emailed Johnie to ask why she had taken on the responsibility of organizing the second conference, she replied, "I now have permission to do so and also the obligation to do it." The impact of what I had been trying to convey to the gold women listening to me as I presented the first time had resonated with Johnie. She understood that the gift of organization given to her by God in her gold personality is something to be used to further His Kingdom. The woman we saw as we entered the doors for that second conference was far different than the woman that I had met at the first conference. Johnie was greeting everyone as they came through the doors and directing all the behind-the-scenes activities that go on to make sure every conference works. I was so happy to see that she had taken my words to the golds to heart.

Be Who God Made You To Be

Our mission as we conduct the color conference is to show

people that they can be the very best that they can be by exhibiting the characteristics of the colors that God made them to be. One of the hardest things we must do in life is "figure out" what God is calling us to do with the unique personalities that He gives us. T.D. Jakes in his book, *Instinct: The Power to Unleash Your Inborn Drive,* says, "Others can inspire you, but ultimately the only thing that empowers you is what lies within you and learning how to better utilize what you've been given."[3] The concepts that we have applied to each personality color can help unlock everyone's ability to discern what God is calling him or her to do.

It is important to note by those who figure out their personality color that no one is all of one color. Those who take our color assessment get a number that tells them how high they rank in each color. The higher the number determines how strongly that individual color dictates how that person operates in the world. Some people test higher in one color, but all of us have some of each color. Generally, the circumstances that you find yourself in determine how your color presents itself. Jesus is a good example of someone who showed others all his colors during his ministry.

We feel that all people are born with either a green, orange, blue, or gold personality color that God gives them. However, we emphasize in our conferences that your second highest color influences your first color. For example, a person who is a gold-orange reacts to situations differently than someone who is gold-green or gold-blue. A gold-orange individual wants order but does not want the order to impede his or her freedom, a gold-green individual wants structure but bases that structure on logic and reason, and the gold-blue individual wants control but wants to make sure that others are not offended in the process. For that reason, it is important that you understand all the personality colors to come to a better understanding of why you see the world as you do.

As the Living Color personality assessment categorizes people into one of only four categories, individuals in each color category will inevitably look different from each other. We know that God has created humans with incredible diversity in so many different areas. We differ in our gender, upbringing, experiences, genetics, work-life, beliefs, values, and so on. It is impossible to perfectly divide people into only four categories. If you read the previous four chapters and thought, "I know what color I am, but I don't fit with everything that's described here," that's okay! We can recognize and celebrate those differences, while also understanding the utility of having this tool that can help us with self-discovery and with approaching those who are different from ourselves.

We have found that some attendees who take our conference assessment will answer the questions such that they are categorized either in the color that aligns with the way they see themselves, the way they think others see them, or the way they want to be perceived. We initially discovered that most middle school students want to be orange when they take the assessment because they want everyone to think they are fun and likable. Sometimes attendees will come up after our presentations and tell us that they now realize that they really are a different color. While taking the assessment, many factors can affect how you answer. Sometimes it is an incorrect perception. Men can admire the green personality because it is perceived as scholarly and not emotional when it really does not represent their personality color. Sometimes the perception is correct, but the individual does not want to be that color. Teachers do not want to be orange because they may not be seen as organized and structured. Men do not want to be seen as emotional and sensitive despite knowing that their blue personality color drives them to connection and relationships. Or finally, the individuals feel like they must be the person that someone has told them to be. Parents can "encourage" a child with a different personality color other than theirs to become more like how the parents think the child should be. In the church setting, people perceive women as nurturing and always seeking a deep connection through specific ministries, but not all women are blue.

On the other hand, while we advocate for everyone to embrace their personality color, your personality color is not a license to forego self-improvement and learning. Once you come to an understanding of the characteristics of your dominant color, you must not make them into a crutch. You CANNOT use your color as your excuse for why you do what you do. For example, someone with a green personality who prefers to work alone cannot make that the reason he or she cannot work with a group. Someone with an orange personality who prefers freedom cannot ignore the rules just to experience that freedom. Someone with a blue personality who does not like conflict cannot ignore an issue until it becomes a real problem. And someone with gold personality cannot fix others' problems by ignoring that the need for control may be the motivation behind the behavior. The excuse that "God made me this way" does not negate the fact that each color must recognize when a dominant personality characteristic turns into a real problem if limits are not applied.

Blending Harmoniously

Those of you who have ever heard a quartet sing in four parts know that you are experiencing something extraordinary when harmony happens. Dr. John Magnuson, the former worship minister and current communications minister at our church, fully understands how harmony is beneficial in a song. He explained, "Great music starts with a simple melody. When you add harmony, the simple melody becomes more interesting and more complete. Harmony helps us tell the whole story. This is consistent with the way that God has always done things. When you can hear the harmony of the other voices and you are singing your part with other people, it gives you confidence and joy. We are not all sopranos, altos, tenor, or basses, but when all those parts are combined, the melody becomes more complex, extraordinary, and ultimately more beautiful."

This comparison of four-part harmony is comparable to the blending of the four color personalities to make something beautiful happen. When each color brings to the table an understanding of the part that is played by that color and uses it in conjunction with the other colors, then the result is something far better than if the color operates by itself. The Living Color team has experienced this.

In our discussion with Dr. Magnuson, he used Paul's analogy of the body parts working together as a metaphor of how the church should be operating. Romans 12:3-6 says, "For by the grace given me I say to every one of you: Do not think of yourself more highly than you ought, but rather think of yourself with sober judgment, in accordance with the measure of faith God has given you. Just as each of us has one body with many members, and these members do not all have the same function, so in Christ, we who are many form one body, and each member belongs to all the others. We have different gifts, according to the grace given us…." As Paul says, we need to value our strengths without elevating ourselves and to see ourselves as an important part of the whole.

Our team understood from the beginning that personality is a gift given to us by God. Psalm 139:14 tells us that we are fearfully and wonderfully made. And Jesus told us that loving each other is second only to loving God (Matthew 22:38-39). Is it easy to love someone else who sees the world through the eyes of a color that is very different from your color? Not always, but it is easier to do just that if you come to an understanding of how that color works. This is the goal of all our color presenters at every one of our conferences. We hope and pray that after reading this book that you walk away with an appreciation of the uniqueness of each color and the value that each color contributes to the world especially when the colors blend harmoniously.

Assembling The Crew

Rhonda's husband Brent has been a builder for over 30 years. In his time, he has seen projects that have worked out beautifully and those that were train wrecks. When discussing the process of building a house, Brent says, "Building projects consist of many tasks, performed by many people. All these different tasks and multiple people need to work together to produce the desired end result." He shares stories about how this job or that job came to a screeching halt because of someone losing sight of the end result. There are keys to success when a project needs to go from plan to product.

One of the keys to completing a project is for everyone to do his or her job and do it well. It starts with the way the foundation is laid. A foundation that is out of line is a recipe for disaster for all the jobs that follow. A person who hangs drywall is counting on the framer to do a good job. A messy framing job makes the job of the drywall hanger so much more difficult because corners don't come out nicely. Pieces must be cut to "make it straight." Fred, the drywall guy, was telling Rhonda how much he appreciated Brent's framing because it made his job so much easier. He said that when he finds out that Brent has framed the house, he breathes a sigh of relief because he knows that the walls are framed correctly. This cadence of one building off the work of the previous job follows all the way until the house is finished.

Another key is to realize that every job has equal importance. Rick, the floor guy, tells of a particular incident when the concrete guys showed up at the job site while his crew was trying to finish these beautiful hardwood floors. Concrete was poured in the garage and both porches, blocking the floor guys from any entryway into the house. They had to crawl through a window to get to their workspace. While each worker should have been complementing the work of others, in this case, progress on the project was impeded. Keeping in mind that you are one of many and being aware of the work that goes on around you keeps the job going smoothly.

Recognizing Your Role On The Jobsite

Similarities emerge when applying these concepts to teams and church settings. Knowing your personality color, recognizing the personality colors of others, and valuing each person's strengths become important for successful Kingdom building. It is a relief to recognize the personality colors of others so that we can understand their actions. Rhonda recalls discovering her daughter's personality color and the clarity it provided. Rhonda had always thought of her daughter Shelby as a "mini-me." Since Rhonda was a blue, she thought that Shelby was blue, too. She definitely exhibited some blue characteristics, but she would not always behave in blue ways. Sometimes, she would prefer silence over pointless chatter. She required time to process information before giving an answer. She was introverted at times. Rhonda thought Shelby's personality was just like hers, so when Shelby went off Rhonda's familiar "blue script," it baffled her.

Rhonda's husband Brent was able to attend one of the Living Color Conferences and took in all the different color talks. The next morning, on the way to church, Brent asked Rhonda, "Hey, have you ever thought that Shelby might be green?" Reflecting on the green talk and comparing it with Shelby, a light turned on. Rhonda thought about it and started crying (because blues cry). It wasn't because Rhonda was sad about Shelby being a green. It was because she had overlooked a key piece in understanding her daughter. All this time, she had assumed that Shelby was a blue. She expected her to act and respond just like Rhonda did. Looking back on certain circumstances, it now made perfect sense to Rhonda. From that time forward, Rhonda embraced, encouraged, and respected the green side of Shelby, knowing that God designed her that way. And when Shelby picked a very green Travis to marry, Rhonda was tickled pink because her Shelby was marrying someone that totally "got" her.

Working Together

Once we recognize each other's personality colors, we can begin to see that our strengths complement other's strengths. Just as the success of each worker on a construction site is contingent on the effectiveness of the others, so is each person within a team dependent, at least in part, on using the strengths of their teammates.

Similarly, Cindy exhibited the strengths of the orange personality when our blue Living Color teammate Rhonda was diagnosed with breast cancer. Caught in the early stages, Rhonda carefully and prayerfully decided, along with her family, that her best option was to have a double mastectomy. Rhonda is a beloved middle school teacher and is known for freely sharing her cell phone number with students along with, "Call me any time—I'm here for you." It's her genuineness and non-judgmental attitude that give her the unique ability to walk alongside students through whatever they are going through. It endears her to all. She shared openly with her students her cancer diagnosis even before many others were aware. As word got out, parents, friends, and colleagues immediately were texting and calling with encouragement, support, and—most importantly—their prayers.

Cindy recognized what her blue friend needed most was to feel wrapped and encouraged with love from all those people who adored her. Dipping into her creative genius pool, Cindy came up with a fun yet tangible way to let Rhonda "feel the love" as she faced this uncertain and anxious time. Why not make Rhonda's cancer journey a little less anxiety-producing by seeing (through that orange filter) an opportunity to combine fun and support into a singular cause? Having taught with Rhonda for many years, Cindy also knew that Rhonda absolutely adored funky and whimsical socks, and everybody wears socks. So, she came up with the unique idea of a sock campaign ("Rhonda's socks") where people could buy and wear coordinating socks on surgery day, March 17, St. Patrick's Day. Multiple emails and selections were made to the small Michigan sock company as many of the styles would sell out with the large quantities ordered. Cindy didn't hesitate to share Rhonda's story with the sock company staff (or anyone else who would listen) because an orange loves sharing story details and encouraging all involved to get on board and share the journey! Cindy's natural gift of banter (she can talk to a wall!) along with humor and a noble motive made sure she got the very best deal (and the cutest socks all with a touch of green). The price of the socks would allow gift cards to be purchased for the Beckhams with funds left over.

"Rhonda's socks" were promoted using Cindy's social media (orange=social!) account, and the support continued to grow even to people who had not met Rhonda but were touched by her story. Many of Rhonda's friends shared Cindy's social media posts so that Rhonda's story could be viewed by many more than just Cindy's friends. So many new messages of encouragement, well-wishes, and prayers were added almost hourly and seen by Rhonda, her husband Brent, and their children. Cindy went to Rhonda's school and set up a table to encourage students, parents, and staff (greet-shouting their name down the hall is a form of "encouragement" by an orange) to purchase Rhonda's socks. EVERYONE wanted to wear "Rhonda's socks" to show solidarity for Mrs. Beckham! Cindy shared later that being at school that day gave her such a sense of connection, purpose, and closeness to Rhonda because of the overwhelming support that was all for her beloved friend. Over 230 pairs of socks were purchased with many people simply making monetary donations in support of the Beckhams.

On surgery day, Rhonda asked that everyone who purchased socks post pictures of themselves and their socks on social media and tag her. What an encouragement it was for Rhonda to see SO many people wearing their "Rhonda's socks" on surgery day…and all for her! A significant number and variety of gift cards were gifted to the Beckhams as a result of the generosity from so many. And Rhonda's friend Cindy took great delight in knowing that by using her orange giftedness of enthusiasm, even in a serious circumstance, and her ability to unify and rally support, she was able to show her blue friend that she was covered in love and solidarity—she was not alone.

Similarly, Debbie has seen different colors using their strengths when working together. Debbie recalls being approached by one of the young mothers at church to start a group for young women so that they could benefit from the interaction with an older woman and with each other. Debbie readily agreed to start the group. When she began planning a lesson for the group each week, Debbie realized how full her gold plate was. She decided to reach out to one of her green friends that she knew was a great Bible teacher to assist her. The green friend was reluctant to assume the responsibility of teaching the group because she feared that the indepth study she would lead would not be what the young women wanted. Debbie told her friend to allow the women to show her whether they appreciated the time and energy that she would devote to the lessons she prepared. It did not take much time before it became evident that the women were absorbing everything that this green teacher was dishing out. Debbie loved to see the women gather on her couch, share a blanket, and wait expectantly for the lesson to unfold as if they were watching the best movie ever. The green teacher brought insight to the lessons that exposed the women to information that no one else had ever shared with them. Often, one of the women would hang around after the study to discuss with Debbie and the green teacher something personal that was happening. Debbie was able to use her gold side to give advice to these women from her past experiences, another strong suit of golds that they enjoy sharing. So, both the green and gold were able to combine their strengths so that everyone got the best of both.

Cindy recalls looking to Debbie's strengths as a gold when she returned to classroom teaching after a seven-year break while raising her children. It was Cindy's first time teaching middle school, and she wanted the most important thing in her classroom to be, "I want you to have fun!" Things didn't go as Cindy had envisioned them. By Christmas, Cindy was in tears in Debbie's guidance counselor's office, humbly asking for help as it seemed the whole year was teetering on disaster! Debbie calmly suggested some ideas to restoring order, and she did not make Cindy feel like a failure by asking for her help! Cindy, in turn, was glad to help Debbie by choosing a wide variety of jewelry when Debbie asked for her creative orange help in accessorizing a few outfits. An orange can aid a gold to be more spontaneous, adventurous, and to color outside the lines. Cindy tells Debbie often that every orange would benefit from having a gold in their life to help them in organizing and focusing on tasks and to assist in formulating a strategy to get there. At some point, all those great ideas and plans that an orange imagines need a course of implementation; a gold is the perfect consultant for that role.

Laura has been a friend of Tiffany's since college. Being green, Tiffany does not divulge all her personal feelings to just anyone. However, being a blue, Laura has always been a safe place for Tiffany to explain emotional and difficult life events. Laura is always empathetic and understanding. Laura and Tiffany have gone through many life stages together—graduating college, getting married, and having children. In addition to much joy, each of these life stages has presented new challenges and difficulties. Laura has always been quick to check-in, text, send a note, or a scripture. Tiffany needed this support, and Laura provided it without even being asked. Additionally, given that Laura is a busy mom with four kids of her own, Laura knows that her relationship with Tiffany is dependable. Blues might sometimes worry about the status of a relationship if the relationship isn't maintained. They may feel disappointed in themselves for not communicating as often as they would like. Tiffany's green allows her to not need as many indicators of connection. For Tiffany, the relationship is always the same no matter how long it takes for them to find time to meet up given their busy schedules. Greens may provide long-lasting friendships for blues despite their many personality differences, and blues are a much-needed source of friendship and comfort for greens.

Intentionally Building Your Team

Oftentimes we find ourselves alongside personality colors that are different from our own. This can translate to situations like those just discussed in which we lean on each other's strengths. Other times, this can be bewildering to find someone so different from ourselves. Rhonda recalls when seven-year-old Allie joined the Beckham family in December 2018. She was unlike anything the Beckhams had experienced. She was spontaneous, competitive, fearless, creative, unfiltered, stubborn, confident; she was very orange. For Rhonda's son Taylor, who is blue/gold, and his wife Chelsey, who is gold/blue, it presented a few hurdles. They had so many questions: Why does she feel the need to talk to EVERYONE? What are we going to do with all of this artwork? What do we do when she wants to leave the house in clothes that don't match? And then there were the questions that were very serious. What do we do? This is where Cindy came to the rescue. Rhonda would call Cindy and tell her the latest Allie story. Through Cindy's orange eyes, the things that Allie did and the way she reacted to different situations made perfect sense. Cindy was able to give advice about how to raise this very orange child. First, Cindy (high orange) knew how Allie (high orange) was processing events and situations. Second, Cindy had the example of her parents, who had given her permission to be orange. What a blessing.

This story with Allie could have ended so differently. If Rhonda's family had not been quick to embrace Allie's differences, Allie could have felt out of place and pressured to act like the rest of the family. If we are willing to embrace the differences of others and recognize how much stronger we are together, then the natural next step is to intentionally build diversity of personality colors into our lives.

Debbie saw this occur firsthand while working at a private Christian school. Her youngest son graduated from high school, and she was feeling a little lost not having an athletic event to attend anymore since she had been attending these events since her sons were in elementary school. One of the green coaches at the school was asked to become the head coach of the high school girls' basketball program. His green personality showed from the beginning in the amount of research and time he would devote to knowing the game and the other teams he would be playing each week. The girls on the team soon learned that the intensity of their green coach taught them life lessons as well as basketball, which resulted in him being asked to perform the weddings of many of his former players. Debbie had never seen anyone "study" the game and his players like he did to be prepared for each game.

Knowing Debbie's strengths as a gold, he asked if she would be his bookkeeper for the games. It became a job that Debbie loved since it involved keeping up with the details of the game. He learned that she could come in handy taking care of other things like helping with fundraisers or taking care of the paperwork that had to be done when they reached the tournament each year. The green coach also recruited one of his orange friends, who had coached at other schools, to assist him. It quickly became apparent that with an orange on board, fun was always around the corner. This orange coach could come up with the most creative ideas that Debbie had ever seen to motivate the girls to play better. Each year brought the girls a locker room experience they would always remember and that showed how the team worked. These two men recognized that they needed a blue personality to be able to help with the emotional needs of high school girls and recruited a blue female friend to assist. The four of them became friends as they learned what each one brought to the mix. It resulted in great memories of the four of them using the strengths of their personality colors to make the team the best that they could be. Debbie learned as she came to understand the personality colors how invaluable it was that each color contributed to the team in ways that fit that color's strength.

Take inventory of the people around you. Likely, you'll recognize multiple personality colors in your life. But if you notice a color is missing, be intentional about discovering a friend with this personality color. You'll be blessed in the process. Likewise, look around your groups. Do you have a team at work composed of all greens and golds? Think about recruiting some blues and oranges. At church, if you notice a ministry team is missing a color, look for someone to fill that role. Our friendships, teams, and churches will be stronger by including different personality colors.

Our Team's Experience

Something special happens when we, as the four color presenters, come together as a team with a true understanding of what each color brings to the table. We discovered early on that going to the family cabin of Cindy, our orange presenter, in the middle of a beautiful country setting was an experience that all of us on the team really treasured. Each team member added something to the mix whether we were planning for a conference or working on the book. Our gold, Debbie, always prepared an agenda to share before we went to keep us all on track, a task that golds delight in doing. She could keep us focused on the task at hand even when our conversations tended to veer away to other subjects. Our orange, Cindy, learned that her creative, artsy side could be used as she would always have a large tablet of paper that could stick to the walls and colored markers to put down any and everything we discussed. These notes were invaluable to us to remember everything we had considered and were posted around the room as the night progressed. Our blue, Rhonda, did not do a lot of talking while she was taking everything in and allowing the others to speak as blues often do, but then she would throw in a nugget that would always change our perspective. We learned to listen. And our green, Tiffany, could expound on a subject with her analytical mind that gave us insight that we always needed. Her scholarly viewpoint was always appreciated, but her green sense of humor (yes, greens have a hilarious side that they share when they feel comfortable in a group) always made us laugh too. We felt the Holy Spirit moving during these times. We respected the strengths of each member of the team, and each one contributed in her own way. No one tried to take over or force her decisions on the others.

The four of us are not "best" friends who hang out together every weekend. But it is a safe place when the four of us are together, and we can freely share. Our levels of assertiveness do not dictate how long each one gets to speak. We do seek out advice from the person who is strong in a color when a problem or situation arises with someone who shares that color. It gives us a broader perspective for when we interact with other colors. We all appreciate when Cindy can explain why an orange is doing something that might not make sense to the other three colors. Or Rhonda can clarify why a blue sees a situation far different in her blue eyes than it is being seen by the gold, green, or orange. Or even when Tiffany explains to us something her green son has done because she understands exactly where he is coming from. We have "lightbulb" moments when you can almost hear the "now I get it" comment from someone on the team because a situation has been explained in our color language that we all understand. We fully understand that the world may look different to each of us but that listening to what the others tell us helps bring clarity to most situations. We truly appreciate what each color adds to our team.

Final Inspection

We often have a natural instinct to wish that people who are different from us were more like ourselves. Wouldn't it be easier to deal with people who think the way you think and behave the way you behave all the time? We could easily predict and understand each other. No more misunderstandings or confusion. However, how much duller and more limited we would all be. We hope that the personality colors presented here encourage you to move from a place of being comfortable in a homogeneous group to wanting to integrate other personality colors into your life. We hope you move from a place of instinctually wanting people to be as gold as you are or as blue as you are into a place of wanting to understand and cooperate with those who are different.

We think that as you begin to recognize your own strengths and the strengths of other colors, you will recognize people in your life who have strengths that would be useful to you. Not only do we want to improve our teams and churches, but we want everyone to have opportunities for growth and learning as they are exposed to other personality colors. We can all learn to have fun and to be spontaneous and flexible from the oranges in our lives. We can all learn to plan, think ahead, and organize from the golds in our lives. We can learn to be sensitive and connected from the blues. And we can learn to be objective and even-handed from the greens. We won't change our personality color (nor should we!), but we can grow through our relationships with other colors.

The theme scripture for our team is I Peter 4:10, "Each one should use whatever gift he has received to serve others, faithfully administering God's grace in its various forms." If you go to the verses that precede this one, you will see that love is the basis for using the gift that you have received. When each of you comes to an understanding of what your gift is according to your personality color, then God allows you to show His grace to the world through the strengths of your personality. David Guzik in his *Enduring Word Bible Commentary* compares God's grace to a ray of light that breaks into a spray of many hues. He says that each of us receives God's grace at a different angle and flashes it back broken up into some fresh color.[4] Our team sees this as a beautiful illustration of the four personality colors. Whether you are green, orange, blue, or gold, show the world God's grace in your life as you show love to others. You can reach us for further information at our website: www.livingcolorconference.com.

Endnotes

1. Pink, D.H. (2018). *When: The Scientific Secrets Of Perfect Timing*. Riverhead Books.
2. Goff, B. (2018). *Everybody Always*. Nelson Books.
3. Jakes, T.D. (2014). *Instinct: The Power To Unleash Your Inborn Drive*. Faith Words.
4. Guzik, D. (2021, May 28). *David Guzik bible commentary on enduring word. Enduring Word*. https://enduringword.com/.

Acknowledgments

We believe that God has had His hand in every aspect of *Colorfully Constructed—How God Builds His Kingdom with Unique Personality Colors* from bringing our team together, to the people He put in our paths, to opening doors and providing opportunities. This book was a work in progress for many years as the four authors figured out what they needed to say about each of their colors. We fully recognize that this book would not have happened without the advice and encouragement that we got from friends and family along the way.

We want to thank David Young who encouraged us to write a book to supplement our Living Color Conferences and gave us advice and direction several times. We greatly appreciate the time he took from his very busy schedule to listen to us. We also must thank Renee Sproles and Danielle Cunningham for pointing us to our newest green presenter, Dr. Tiffany Rogers, by telling us that she would make a great team addition with her green insight. We would also like to thank Bonnie Blaylock for taking on her role as our editor to get this book ready for publication. She gave us invaluable advice on changes that needed to be made and wisdom on preparing this book for publication. We have a special place in our hearts for our attorney, Lynn Watson, who met with us to advise us on the legal aspects of the writing process.

The North Boulevard Church of Christ staff have supported us in ways that has made this journey happen. Megan Starling, our graphic designer, put our graphics into actual designs and gave us her wisdom on our website. She designed our book cover with her creative vision. Mike Jones helped us with our visuals, and William Cavataio helped with our website design and the conference registration process. Tom Beckwith, our favorite orange photographer, was always willing to come to take photos of us at a moment's notice. John Magnuson has supported us with speaking opportunities along the way and perspectives on his color. Joe Roberts provided direction on our ministry expenses and editing process.

The team saw it as a "God-thing" when Abby Rosser unexpectedly joined us while we were meeting one day to organize a conference and suggested we talk to her book publisher at WordCrafts Press. Abby was so good to guide us in the process of getting this book to our publisher, Mike Parker. He has been wonderful to work with as we have navigated the process of publishing our first book. You would not be reading this book without his faith in us to produce something that would be appealing to all who pick it up.

We must thank all the people out there who believed enough in what we were doing to allow us to come to their church or organization to tell them about personality colors. It began with Nancy Hatton who first called asking us to present at our home congregation. Kelley Mullins and Penny Vick started us on this road with their early requests for presentations. We appreciate all the work that went into making our conferences happen from Kristin Turner, Yvonne Clark, Johnie Bischell, Jenny Nance, Linda Smock, Jennifer Brewer, Amy Marcus, Karen Lonis, Jeri Dearden, Michelle Scherer, Caroline Scherer, and Beth Watson. We have loved going to Lipscomb University to present to the nursing students thanks to Kathy Williams.

We will always be grateful to our first presenters, Lynne Maxwell and Vicki Kennedy, who helped us forge our way to where we are now. Their insights into each of their personality colors opened the eyes of so many who heard them speak.

Our husbands have listened to us, encouraged us, allowed us to travel, and been there for us when we needed them. Carolyn Perry has become our "team Mom" and has always given us encouragement and loving words of support. God has blessed us in ways that we never imagined when we first came together as a team. The Holy Spirit has led us on this path, and we pray that our words are His words. Our desire has always been that each of you will use whatever personality that God has given you to serve others as I Peter 4:10 tells us. Thank you for reading this book!

Biographies

Rhonda Beckham

After 20 years as a stay-at-home mom, Rhonda returned to school to earn her bachelor's degree in education from Lipscomb University. She teaches all things history and geography to middle school minds and loves her job—most days. She and her husband Brent have been married for over 30 years and live on a quiet piece of land in Rockvale, where she loves to sit on her back porch with her side-kick Sophie. While Sophie, a small Yorkie-poo, protects and guards the perimeter, Rhonda prays, studies, naps, reads, and watches the wildlife from this special spot. Her son Taylor and his wife Chelsey live near Atlanta with the grandest of grands, Allie and Summit. Their "Nana" cannot get enough of them. Rhonda's daughter Shelby and her husband Travis live in Nashville. Rhonda's happiest of places is anytime spent with these folks. They keep her bucket filled with hugs, laughter, food, and beautiful noise. Rhonda uses the insight gained from the Living Color Conferences to understand and make better connections to those around her, including students, colleagues, friends, and even family.

Debbie Mankin

Debbie has a bachelor's degree in education from Lipscomb University and a master's degree in counseling from Liberty University. She owned and operated her own business in her home for 13 years while raising her two sons. She then worked in the education field for 22 years as a teacher, guidance counselor, and administrative assistant before retiring in 2019. As a guidance counselor, Debbie used insight from the Living Color Conference to help her guide students and teachers into a better understanding of themselves, their family, and their peers. Since then, she has shared this tool with churches throughout the Southeast. Through these conferences and her walk as a wife for more than 40 years and grandmother to three wonderful grandchildren, Debbie has felt God leading her to discover that He has a plan for her, her family, and each of you. Debbie enjoys reading and leading her church small groups when she is not organizing the next Living Color Conference.

Cindy Patton

Cindy received her bachelor's and master's degrees in education from Middle Tennessee State University with stops along the way at Lipscomb University and the University of Hawaii. She retired in 2019 following 17 years of teaching mostly middle school math and Bible. Married for over 40 years to her high school sweetheart, Peter, she is mom to four amazing Christ-following adult children, mother-in-law to two incredible sons-in-love, and "Boo" to her six most precious grandchildren! She enjoys creating ("fun, not fine") art, sewing, going on mission trips, spending time with family and friends at "the cabin," teaching and speaking to teen and women's groups, and claiming the self-appointed title of "best chocolate-chip cookie maker!" Cindy feels the concepts learned from the Living Color Conference have given her "permission" to be the person she was wired to be and have reminded her how to value and appreciate each of our "varied gifts" while serving in God's Kingdom.

Dr. T.D. Rogers

Tiffany received her bachelor's degree in Psychology from Lipscomb University in 2006. She then received her master's degree (2009) in Experimental Psychology and her doctoral degree (2012) in Behavioral Neuroscience from the University of Memphis. She worked as a postdoctoral fellow at Vanderbilt University researching neurodevelopmental disorders from 2012 to 2015. Tiffany has since worked at Middle Tennessee State University teaching neuroscience and research-related courses and running a neuroscience research lab on campus. She and her husband have been married for 12 years, and they have three young children. She enjoys spending time with her family, gardening, crafting, and adding to a long list of short-term hobbies primarily taken up just to learn something new.

Made in the USA
Columbia, SC
11 July 2022

63201495R00059